ideas

BERESHIT

SINA KAHEN

ideas

BERESHIT

IDEAS
Bereshit

First Edition, 2020

©Sina Kahen, 2020

ISBN 9798656078269

www.SinaKahen.com

Reviews and approbations

In his 'Ideas', Sina Kahen skilfully reminds us through a consistent and prolific display that Torah is meant to be for us a lens through which we see, interpret, and understand the entire world. There is no aspect of this world or the human condition that Torah does not discuss in deep, relevant, and meaningful ways. In this pertinent work, Sina shows us brief examples of the nature of this system. He points out that this system is not exclusive to, but it is central and predominant in, Western Sephardi Torah scholarship. It is with much pride and joy that I recommend this book to all who wish to have a sense of how Torah has been applied and can be applied to even the most current and cutting-edge issues and questions. To read his pages is to take first steps into seeing the Torah's broad embrace of all aspects of God's creation.

RABBI JOSEPH DWECK
Senior Rabbi, The S&P Sephardi Community, United Kingdom

In these essays, Sina beautifully weaves quotations from all sorts of Jewish sources, ancient and modern, which join in forming a mosaic of ideas and lessons very relevant to modern society and the challenges we face. Sina's book demonstrates yet again how our Torah serves as fountain of knowledge, guidance, and morality for every generation. I am sure this book will find favour in the eyes of all its readers, and hope that Sina will continue to write and publish further books bringing to light the profound ideas of the Torah and our Sages.

DAYAN OFER LIVNAT
The Sephardi Beth Din, United Kingdom

The Golden Age of Spanish Jewry spanned several centuries in the Iberian Peninsula. During much of that time, Torah study and intellectual inquiry were heavily influenced by the Islamic parent culture, which viewed itself as the torchbearer for Greek philosophy, particularly the Aristotelian and Neoplatonic variety. This influence is most manifest in the writings of Maimonides, but can also be found in so many other Jewish writers of the time. This period left an indelible imprint on the world of Jewish thought for Jews worldwide, not just for Sephardic Jews. Sina Kahen, like so many other Sephardic Jews who relate to this rational, intellectual approach to Judaism, has taken up this mantle of his heritage. Through a lens of both medieval and modern authors from this school of thought, he provides innovative approaches to various ideas, mitzvot, and narratives found in the weekly Torah portion. His insights are profound, but also terse and straightforward enough to discuss at your Shabbat table with friends and family. His writing is a valuable contribution to the catalogue of Jewish literature of this genre. May you glean much wisdom from his book.

RABBI N. DANIEL KOROBKIN
President, The Rabbinical Council of America

As most are aware, scholars throughout Jewish history have offered various approaches as to how one should interpret the Torah. There have been interpreters who focused on the simple meaning (peshat), and others who focused on midrashic or mystical insights. One important trend in the history of Torah interpretation has unapologetically incorporated general knowledge in seeking to understand God's word. For the advocates of this approach, who include many great figures from the medieval period time until the present, God's wisdom can be seen not only in the words of the Torah, but also through the achievements of human intellect. Some point to science and philosophy while others claim that all areas of intellectual endeavor, in particular the study of history and literature, allow us to better appreciate the Torah's message in all of its timelessness. In his new work on Bereshit, Sina Kahen follows the approach of these sages to offer us profound insights on the weekly Torah portion. The authors he cites span the globe and eras of Jewish history. On account of certain historical reasons, many today are unaware of how these great Torah scholars, each in his own way, created a synthesis of what has often been called "Torah and intellect". Kahen takes his place in this great tradition and we can look forward to future instalments of his work on the other books of the Torah.

RABBI PROFESSOR DR MARC SHAPIRO
Author of 'Studies in Maimonides', 'Changing the Immutable'

Sina Kahen hasn't just written a book; he has curated a conversation, punctuated with choice quotes from a diverse cast of sages and thinkers. Readers are invited to take part in that conversation, to agree, or to disagree; to meditate on the many themes and ideas, and to see what new insights they can generate on their own. A *fine example in the long tradition, too often neglected, of enlightened, open-minded, fearless, faithful, and distinctively Sephardi Torah.*

RABBI DR SAMUEL LEBENS
Philosophy Department, University of Haifa

Whilst the Torah is the Jewish people's bedrock, Judaism recognises that there is much wisdom to be derived from outside the walls of the Bet Hamidrash. By beautifully weaving together passages from both Jewish and non-Jewish sources in his masterful work, Ideas, Sina Kahen gives us a cogent and well-rounded understanding of the book of Bereshit. His 'ideas' relate to the core of our human existence: love, speech, creativity, self-discovery, identity and transcendence. Despite their depth and profundity, Kahen's essays are shareable and relatable. One who needs any proof of the relevance of the Torah in the 21st century, need look no further than this wonderful book. I hope the author will continue to write and inspire thinking Jews.

DAYAN DANIEL KADA
The Sephardi Beth Din, United Kingdom

This is certainly an unusual and eclectic work. The author believes in a Judaism of the mind as well as the heart. He confidently weaves together ideas from scholars both within and beyond the Jewish tradition, but is especially enamoured of his own Sephardic tradition whose richness and profundity has so much to contribute to our understanding of the Torah today. If you want to go on an intellectual adventure, read this book.

RABBI DR RAPHAEL ZARUM
Dean, The London School of Jewish Studies

Sina Kahen has done something remarkable. He has drawn on clear thinking, modern insight, and a wealth of sources to provide insights into the Torah portions of Bereshit. This work will challenge readers not only to study the text more carefully...but to think more carefully on basic issues of religion and life.

RABBI DR MARC D. ANGEL
Director, Institute for Jewish Ideas and Ideals
Emeritus Senior Rabbi, The Spanish & Portuguese Jews, New York

As Honorary Principal of the Judith Lady Montefiore College, I welcome this short but meaningful book which reflects so well the ethos of our numerous projects. I look forward to the future volumes of this series.

RABBI DR ABRAHAM LEVY O.B.E.
Emeritus Senior Rabbi, The Spanish & Portuguese Jews, London

It is an immense honor for me to write these brief words sharing my impressions of "Ideas" on Bereshit, the handiwork of my dear friend R' Sina Kahen, may HaKadosh Baruch Hu bless him with a long and healthy life. In these pages, R' Sina shares with us refreshing and relevant insights on the weekly Torah portion, weaving together extremely varied sources to create convincing Jewish ideas which engage and give reasons to the educated, intelligent Jew. Among the diverse rabbis and scholars presented within this book, it is especially exciting for me to see the names of the greatest of the Sages of Sepharad, exposing English-speaking Torah learners to their life-changing words of wisdom, full of clarity and truth. R' Sina has not only single-handedly restored their honor and dignity so that these giants shall not be forgotten by the apathy shown towards them by the Judaism of today, he has also faithfully followed in their footsteps and continued to expound on the Torah in ways which would make them proud, especially our Master and Teacher the Rambam, peace be upon him, who taught us to "accept the truth from whomever says it". As such, R' Sina has merited to take his rightful place alongside the great minds of our illustrious tradition, and about him it must be said: "fortunate is she who gave birth to him". I am left only to bless him that he may continue to publish more works in the likeness of this one, b'ezrat HaBoreh Yitbarach.

RABBI YONATAN HALEVY
Founder, Shiviti
Spiritual Leader, Kehillat Shaar HaShamayim

Sina Kahen has provided us with a set of clear and concise core principles of rationalist Jewish thought built on an impressive array of earlier sources. A valuable contribution to Torah literature.

RABBI SHMUEL PHILLIPS
Author of 'Judaism Reclaimed'

I have looked over the work for R' Sina Kahen, in his book Ideas on Sefer Bereshit. While I regret to only have had the time for a cursory review of what he has written, he has done an impressive job of taking from the wisdom of our sages throughout the ages, and fusing them together to create a complete whole. To all this he adds, of course, his own personal flavor. I hope that many will find the short, clear ideas in this book inspiring and thought-provoking, and wish the author the strength and wisdom to continue to produce such and other works in the future.

RABBI YONATAN ROSENSWEIG

Rabbi, Netzah Menashe Community, Beit Shemesh
Emeritus Rosh Yeshiva, Yeshivat Hamivtar & Yeshivat Shevut Yisrael

Contents

To Talya, Noa, and Joseph.
My reasons.

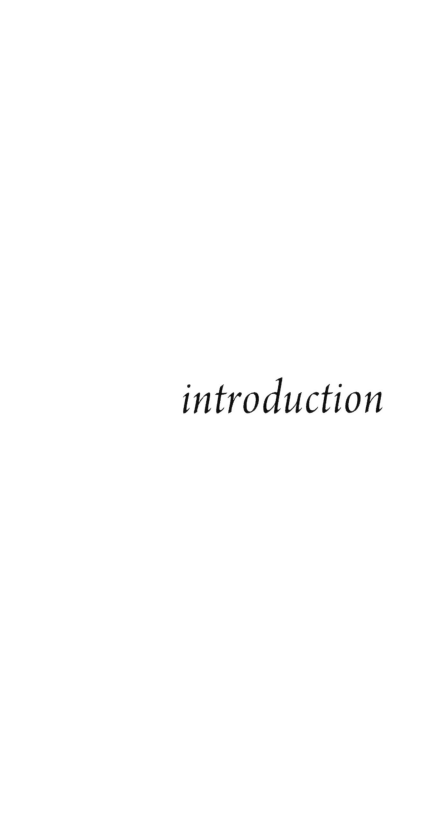

introduction

To grasp as much of the truth as is humanly possible, man must lay the whole realm of knowledge under honour.

In gathering this knowledge, he must be willing to learn from all, whether they be of high or low status, whether they be members of his own faith or belong to other faiths, whether they be believers or infidels.

In the providence of learning, as in the field of practical everyday living, we should break the nut open, enjoy the meat, and discard the shell.*

HAKHAM YA'AKOV ANATOLI

Introduction

The human brain has a distinct ability to think hierarchically.

This means that it can understand a structure formed by different elements arranged in a pattern, go on to represent that arrangement with a symbol, and then use that symbol as a component in an even more elaborate structure.

These patterns are what we call *ideas*.

> *Ideas are things grasped by the mind, and sensible things are, in some sense, derived from them.*[1]
>
> PLATO

Through an endlessly recursive process, we are capable of building ideas that are ever more complex. This vast assortment of recursively linked ideas is referred to as *knowledge*.

Only Homo sapiens has a seat of knowledge that can evolve, develop exponentially, and be shared from one generation to another. An idea from yesterday can become the reality of tomorrow.

> *When an idea is born in this world, it does not remain unfulfilled, but it travels through space until it finds an incubator in which to develop, it grows skin and muscle and becomes a reality.*[2]
>
> HAKHAM YOSEF QAFIH

The ideas gleaned from the weekly portions of our Torah (*perashat hashavua*) have enlightened and advanced human civilisation.

---

* Ya'akov Anatoli, *Malmad haTalmidim*, Vaera p. 49a; Pinhas p. 150b

[1] Adapted from Plato, *Parmenides*, 132b

[2] Yosef Qafih, Introduction to Rambam's *Mishneh Torah*

> *"A golden candelabrum" (Zekhariah 4:2)*
>> *– This is Yisrael. Just as the candle illuminates the house,*
>> *so Yisrael illuminates the entire world by means of the*
>> *Torah.*[3]
>
> HAKHAM SHELOMO AL-RABIAH

As mankind first laid its eyes on this divine text, ideas were brought out from it to form a running commentary that has lasted over 2000 years.

> *Just as a hammer breaks a stone into several fragments, so too,*
> *one verse is stated by God and from it emerge several*
> *explanations.*[4]
>
> TALMUD BAVLI

Much ink has been spilled in analysing the Torah, and much blood has been spilled in defending it. Yet, the well remains as full and nourishing as ever, waiting for the next idea to be carried up from it to satiate those near and far.

> *Come, all who are thirsty, come for water!*[5]
>
> YESHAYAHU

At their very core, ideas are ultimately the precursors to developing and preparing for our life, our world, and our legacy.

> *Rabbi Yehoshua said to his students, "What novel idea was*
> *taught today in the study hall?"*[6]
>
> TALMUD BAVLI

> *A person should engage all his days in matters of wisdom and*
> *in the ordering of the world.*[7]
>
> RAMBAM

---

[3] Shelomo Ben Shalom Yadia Al-Rabiah, *Derash haMazhir* (Available in Tzvi Langermann, *Yemenite Midrash*, p. 239)

[4] Sanhedrin 34a

[5] Yeshayahu 55:1

[6] Hagigah 3a

[7] Rambam, *Mishneh Torah*, Hilkhot Gezelah vaAvedah 6:11

> *This world is a passageway before the world to come; prepare*
> *yourself in the passageway, so that you may enter the*
> *banqueting-hall.*[8]
>
> PIRKEI AVOT

The ideas expressed in this book are not exclusively mine. Rather, they are implicitly (and more often explicitly) influenced by a legion of *hakhamim* who generated ideas that are intellectually honest and spiritually fulfilling.

These include *hakhamim* such as Rambam, Meiri, Radak, Rabbenu Bahya, Ramhal, Rivash, Ralbag, Ri Migash, Ibn Ezra, Nissim Gerondi, Sa'adia Gaon, Hoter ben Shelomo, Ya'akov Anatoli, Ibn Kaspi, Nissim ben Moshe, Ibn Tibbon, Yosef Albo, Zekhariah ben Rofe, Elia Del Medigo, Ben Zion Uziel, Shimshon Raphael Hirsch, David Nieto, Avraham Yitzhak Kook, Joseph Soloveitchik, Aharon Lichtenstein, Yosef Qafih, Yosef Faur, Jonathan Sacks, Joseph Dweck, Eliezer Melamed, Moshe Shamah, and others.

While some of these *hakhamim* and their ideas may already be known to the reader, there will be many that, sadly, will not[9] – until now.

These *hakhamim* range from Talmudic times, to current times; from Spain and Yemen, to the UK and the USA; from insular enclaves, to outward-facing communities. The one constant that these *hakhamim* share, however, is that their ideas on the Torah are enriched through their knowledge and appreciation of God's other fingerprints: science, philosophy, art, history, and more. These *hakhamim* developed patterns of thought that are held together by these diverse threads of knowledge, in order to aid in the illumination of Torah and in the apprehension of God.

> *And what branch of human wisdom is there that can be*
> *ignored in our efforts to arrive at a fuller knowledge of God?*[10]
>
> HAKHAM YA'AKOV ANATOLI

---

[8] Pirkei Avot 4:16

[9] Due to political, sociological, and historical reasons that go beyond the remit of this book. I recommend the reader to search and research each and every person quoted in this book.

[10] Ya'akov Anatoli, *Malmad haTalmidim*, Vaet'hanan, p. 159b

The apprehension of God cannot come about except through divine science [metaphysics], and this cannot become actual except after a study of natural science.[11] *A human being has to set himself aside to come to understand through understanding science, the world, things that teach him about God, to the maximum that a human being is capable of.*[12]

RAMBAM

[The contribution of general knowledge] to the elucidation of Torah is just that: it enhances, enriches, illuminates, adds information and insights; extends dimensions of clarity, range, and depth.[13]

RABBI AHARON LICHTENSTEIN

By means of the Torah, the great value of all the secular wisdoms and all the productivity made to improve the world, are revealed.[14]

RABBI ELIEZER MELAMED

It is impossible to understand Torah – certainly to plumb its depths – without a profound and broad knowledge of all worldly wisdoms and sciences.[15] *'Talmud Torah' is a general term referring to the attainment of wisdom; it includes Torah study as well as all the studies and sciences which deepen our understanding.*[16] *Our holiness will only be complete if we are nourished by all the new developments in the world, by all the wonderous discoveries, by all the philosophical and scientific ideas which flourish and multiply in our world.*[17]

HAKHAM BEN ZION UZIEL

---

[11] Rambam, *Moreh haNevukhim*, Introduction

[12] Rambam, *Mishneh Torah*, Hilkhot Teshuva 10:6

[13] Aharon Lichtenstein, *Torah and General Culture: Confluence and Conflict*, p. 291.

[14] Eliezer Melamed, *The Value of Torah and of Secular Wisdom*, Besheva Newspaper, 13th March 2020. Available online: https://revivimen.yhb.org.il/

[15] Ben Zion Uziel, *Mikhmanei Uziel*, p. 405

[16] Ibid. p. 552-553

[17] Ben Zion Uziel, *Hegyonei Uziel*, Volume 2, p. 133-134

These *hakhamim* serve as a warm light to future generations, by articulating an intellectual vision of life that sees the Torah and the world around it as integrated partners, not as inevitable opponents. By committing to this holistic approach, they are fulfilling Yisrael's core obligation to love God.[18]

> *"And you shall love the Lord your God." (Devarim 6:5)*
> *— What is the path to loving Him? Upon one's contemplation of His works [Torah] and His great and wonderful creations [science, nature, etc.], discovering in them His endless and limitless wisdom, one comes directly to love and to praise, glorify and yearn with a great desire to know Him.[19]*
>
> RAMBAM

These are *hakhamim* for whom intellect rather than prejudice, ideas and realities rather than superstition and fancy, form the natural background of their vision of Torah and its divine message.

It is for this reason that I have quoted these unique *hakhamim* alongside unique thinkers from other nations who have also expressed ideas that reinforce many Torah ideas. The thoughtful contributions from the wisdom of other nations, which are presented in the form of quotations throughout the book, serve to highlight the universal relevance of many Torah ideas.

> *For Torah, which is the heritage of the congregation of Ya'akov, implies more than a body of ancient religious wisdom; it also signifies a particular method of approach, such a minute study and careful probing of the truth embodied in the text as will disclose its deeper meaning and wider application.[20]*
>
> HAKHAM YA'AKOV ANATOLI

---

[18] As David Berger eloquently states in *Judaism's Encounter with Other Cultures*, p. 97: *"If love of God, clearly a quintessential religious value, was to have any real meaning, it could only flow from a knowledge of the Creator's handiwork, and this required a pursuit of the sciences."*

[19] Rambam, *Mishneh Torah*, Hilkhot Yesodei haTorah 2:1-2

[20] Ya'akov Anatoli, *Malmad haTalmidim*, Vayhi, p. 44

This holistic approach is similar, but different, to the model of thought commonly known today as *Torah u-Madda* (Torah and "secular" knowledge), which attempts to bridge gaps between Torah and worldly knowledge, arguing for their peaceful coexistence. After all, there is nothing "secular" about any knowledge or truth that describes God's world.

> *The perfect Torah is that which brings all sciences to perfection.*[21]
>
> HAKHAM HOTER BEN SHELOMO

> *All those subjects and sciences which, for some reason, people refer to as "secular knowledge", if a person studies them in order to arrive at insight and knowledge of God – behold, they are surely sacred.*[22]
>
> HAKHAM YOSEF QAFIH

> *The signature of God is Truth.*[23]
>
> TALMUD BAVLI

When the content of our world is seen through this context of Torah, it becomes clear that the truths derived from all areas of worldly knowledge are simply the *effects*, and God is the *Cause*.

> *Man's intellectual research proceeds from the effect to the cause.*[24]
>
> HAKHAM YITZHAK ARAMA

Indeed, for many of these *hakhamim*, studying these areas of knowledge through the lens of Torah was even considered the pinnacle of their experiences with God, and their attempts to know Him.[25]

---

[21] Hoter ben Shelomo, *Siraj al-Uqul* (Available in Tzvi Langermann, *Yemenite Midrash*, p. 229)

[22] Yosef Qafih, *Ketavim*, Volume 2, p. 594

[23] Yoma 69b

[24] Yitzhak Ben Moshe Arama, *Akedat Yitzhak*, 45:1:7

[25] Although one can never know the *essence* of God, one can still know Him through His ways and expressions (*derakhim*) such as Torah, science, and the other details (*peratim*) of reality that He presents us with. Similarly, you can never know the *essence* of another person, but you

> *If we are to enter into His innermost abode, we shall scale the heights of the natural sciences, assured that at the summit we shall find Him.*[26]
>
> HAKHAM YA'AKOV ANATOLI

> *The whole universe is perceived as a semiological entity that "points out toward Him."*[27]
>
> HAKHAM YOSEF FAUR

THE FEAR OF INTELLECT

The post-religious world we find ourselves in can only lead us to conclude that "pop" (popular) religion does not suffice in providing the answers to our generation's primal need for comprehension, and it cannot survive a developing world.

> *Popular religion is not intelligent enough to benefit by the infiltration of new ideas.*[28]
>
> HAKHAM YA'AKOV ANATOLI

Indeed, this "pop" religion is firmly rooted in the realm of the imagination.

> *The young and the general public inhabit the realm of imagination. Because the key-symbols that give coherence to the general public are grounded on imagination, the public is unable to think in terms of reason and will remain totally blind throughout its earthly existence.*[29]
>
> HAKHAM YOSEF FAUR

Most of us will begin our lives relying on our imagination, as we simply do not know how things in the world around us work. Similarly, "pop" religion relies upon this inferior faculty of imagination to aid in our understanding of

---

can know that person through the expressions and persona they put out. See Rambam, *Moreh haNevukhim*, Part 1, Chapter 34 for an analysis of this important point.

[26] Ya'akov Anatoli, *Malmad haTalmidim*, Bo, p. 54a

[27] Jose Faur, *Homo Mysticus*, p. 101

[28] Ya'akov Anatoli, *Malmad haTalmidim*, Introduction; Bereshit, p. 3a; Vaera, p. 51a

[29] Jose Faur, *Homo Mysticus*, p. 58

religion. A prime example of the need for this imaginative faculty is evident in the Torah's description of God as having bodily parts and emotions (anthropomorphism), as a way for humanity to try and relate to Him.

However, the "pop" religion of recent times has created an unhealthy imagination rooted in a series of lazy distinctions such as Torah vs secular knowledge, rationality vs mysticism, intellect vs experience, knowledge vs faith.

These false dichotomies are created because compartmentalisation and binarisation offer us a false sense of security. In other words, we prefer to pick a side in order to allay our most powerful primal emotion – fear.

The fear of finding a contradiction, the fear of not finding a solution, the fear of disbelief. These are all, fundamentally, the fear of intellect.

The outcome of such fear leaves behind a vacuum of knowledge that is ultimately filled in by the illegitimate child of imagination, the arch nemesis of intellect – superstition.

> *Fear is the main source of superstition.*[30]
>
> BERTRAND RUSSELL

As such, "pop" presentations of Torah can deny mature minds the ability to consciously utilise our unique and divine intellectual capabilities in the exploration of Torah's truth.

Logic – that glorious God-given gem – has been plucked from its' place on the crown of Torah.

> *The truth has evaded some of the commentators, for they are ignorant of the science of logic, and even if some of them do know it, they do not remember its foundations when they comment.*[31]
>
> YOSEF IBN KASPI

---

[30]Bertrand Russell, *Unpopular Essays,* 'An Outline of Intellectual Rubbish'
[31] Yosef Ibn Kaspi, *Commentary on Esther,* p. 31

It is certain to us that through logic, Torah, and tradition, we are obligated to speculate upon every matter the truth of which is conceivable to our minds.[32]

RABBENU BAHYA

It is certainly necessary for whoever wishes to achieve human perfection to first train himself in the art of logic.[33]

RAMBAM

While many "pop" presentations of fast-food Torah can trigger moments of temporary meaning and contentment, and even provide entry-points for otherwise uninterested Jews to explore and fulfil their divine mission, the mature mind inevitably grows out of it.

Still, we must be under no illusions. Just as there can be *too little* intellectual rigour and investigation, so too can there be *too much* – especially without the proper intention.

We cannot always rely upon the conclusions of the mind; and since knowledge divorced from piety can endure for a while, we must never allow ourselves to treat lightly the principles and injunctions of the Torah. Independent study and investigation are eminently worthwhile, if they be motivated by a desire to build up and not to destroy.[34]

HAKHAM YA'AKOV ANATOLI

And of course, we cannot ignore that which goes beyond the realm of the rational – the realm of the *supra*-rational.[35] Here, we are faced with a crisis of

---

[32] Bahya Ibn Paquda, *The Duties of the Heart*, Chapter 1, p. 115

[33] Rambam, *Moreh haNevukhim*, 1:34

[34] Ya'akov Anatoli, *Malmad haTalmidim*, Vaera, p. 49b

[35] Supra-rationality is defined as that which transcends rationality and is incomprehensible by human reason alone. This should *never* be equated with irrationality (the quality of being illogical or unreasonable). The lack of a clear distinction between supra-rationality and irrationality has influenced much of the decay in rational thought among contemporary Jewish belief and practice.

knowledge as we arrive at the edge of our intellectual capacity. To fail to respect this limit is to be reckless.

> *"They should not recklessly go up to the Lord." (Shemot 19:24)*
>> *– In case they rush and extend their thoughts to that which is beyond their capacity. People who engage in inquiry and rational demonstrations fix a boundary for their intellects.*[36]
>>> HAKHAM ZEKHARIAH ROFE

> *Discussion of that which is beyond human comprehension is logically absurd.*[37]
>> THE MEIRI

> *Reason is insulted when its careless practitioners fail to recognise its limitations.*[38]
>> MARK HELPRIN

So, what is left beyond our capacity to reason? What can we turn to when rationality can only take us so far?

The human experience.

> *Know, my masters, that it is not proper for a man to accept as trustworthy anything other than one of these three things:*
> *The first is a thing for which there is a clear proof deriving from man's reasoning.*
> *The second is a thing that a man perceives through one of the five senses* [EXPERIENCE].
> *The third is a thing that a man receives from the Prophets or from the righteous.*[39]
>> RAMBAM

---

[36] Zekhariah ben Shelomo Rofe, *Midrash haHefes*, Shemot 19:24
[37] Menahem Meiri, *Perush Mishle*, 21:30-1, p. 213. This is referenced in Gregg Stern, *Philosophy and Rabbinic Culture*, p. 124
[38] Mark Helprin, *New Threats to Freedom*, p. 106
[39] Rambam, *Letter to the Community of Marseille (Letter on Astrology)*

Therefore, beyond the edge of reason, we arrive at supra-rational *experiences* that consist of emergent and non-physical properties.

Indeed, the existence of an emergent phenomenon (such as the experience of *love*) is vastly more complex than, and cannot be predicted nor created by, its constituent parts (such as *oxytocin, dopamine,* or *vasopressin*).

Furthermore, *to reduce it is to lose it.* Nothing dulls the synapses of emergent experiences more depressingly than cynical reductionism – the modus operandi of Scientism.[40]

> *It would be possible to describe everything scientifically, but it would make no sense; it would be without meaning, as if you described a Beethoven symphony as a variation of wave pressure.*[41]
>
> ALBERT EINSTEIN

This is not only true for love, but is also the case for other emergent and meta-physical phenomena such as mysticism, faith, and imagination.

In other words, our *intellectual* tools are limited in their grasp of existence. While *intellectual* tools can be used to penetrate and dissect the realities of the physical world, we obtain a different set of *experiential* tools to grasp emergent and meta-physical phenomena. The need for *experiential* tools becomes evident once one tries (and fails) to describe colour to a blind person.

And at once we acknowledge the dual nature of our being.

Nonetheless – and this is critical – we must not have mysticism, faith, nor imagination emerge from *weak* physical, rational, and intellectual foundations. Unfortunately, this has become the norm for many religious

---

[40] Scientism is the reduction of all knowledge to that of the scientific form. It is a dark and religious by-product of the Enlightenment that exploits the honour of science in areas that are beyond its remit.

[41] Albert Einstein, as quoted in Max Born, *Physik im Wandel meiner Zeit.* (Braunschweig: Vieweg, 1966)

people. For example, some hold tight to the belief that an emergent entity such as faith must be in *opposition* to reality, rather than *beyond* it – the difference between *irrational* faith and *supra-rational* faith.[42] Although supra-rational faith leaps beyond external evidence, it is not groundless. Irrational faith, however, is groundless, illogical, and specious. Some go so far as to believe that the further their faith takes them *away* from reality, the closer they are to piety and Truth. We cannot doubt the sincerity of those who think this way, but a hint of arrogance may lay behind such an ideological position. After all, it implies that they are exclusively entitled to interpret Torah as something that must blind us from the realities that God expresses, rather than help clarify and address them.

Therefore, a healthy and viable mysticism, faith, and imagination can only emerge from an accurate understanding of the physical reality around us. In other words, the surrounding data we input through our senses must be received by a thought-processor that is rationally sound.

> *Reason alone is static and unproductive... But imagination alone is deceiving and destructive.*[43]
> HAKHAM YOSEF FAUR

Indeed, the troubles caused by an imagination running riot have long been established.

> *The word 'satan' in Hebrew (literally 'deceiver') stems from the root 'sata' ('to deviate, to stray from the right path'), implying a distorted image of reality produced by the imaginative faculty... Adam fell prey to his "imaginary desires", sinning by losing his rational grasp of reality.*[44]
> HAKHAM YOSEF FAUR

This risk is, in part, a consequence of an ongoing struggle between the *left-side* of the brain (responsible for logic and rationality), and the *right-side* of

---

[42] See footnote 35.
[43] Jose Faur, *Homo Mysticus*, p. 72
[44] Ibid. p. 62

the brain (responsible for emotion and imagination). Although recent research has shown the confluence of both regions and the faculties that emerge from them, the *right-side* has had a historical tendency to lure us away from reality!

> *Satan was standing to his RIGHT, to lead him astray.*[45]
>
> ZEKHARIAH

Therefore, the rational mind must be utilised to challenge the superstitious and irrational ideas of an unfettered religious imagination that ultimately leads to shortcuts instead of relationship *(berit)*, to falsehood *(sheker)* instead of truth, and strange worship *(avodah zarah)* instead of proper service – even if they are cloaked in the garb of piety.

> *The deception is so great that even the best of the faithful among our scholars of Torah think that they are true. They do not realise that they are nonsensical false things that the Torah warned against, just as it warned us against falsehoods.*[46]
>
> RAMBAM

> *The failure to accept that God alone provides for man drives Jews to seek an imagined security by wearing red strings, checking Mezuzahs, carrying Jewish books for protection, praying to the dead, paying for human blessings, and performing acts at certain times and with certain objects.*[47]
>
> RABBI MOSHE BEN-CHAIM

Logic is a divine tool that must be used to dissipate these dominating clouds of intellectual darkness amongst Yisrael, persistently thickened by *"clogged minds, who are devoted to superstitious nonsense and immersed in the fetid waters of unilluminated caves."*[48]

---

[45] Zekhariah 3:1

[46] Rambam, *Commentary to the Mishnah,* Avodah Zarah 4:7

[47] Moshe Ben-Chaim, *Judaism: Religion of Reason,* Introduction, p. 10

[48] Radak, *Qovez Teshuvot haRambam,* 3b

Ideas

> While we preach the doctrines of God's law, let us cling with
> devotion to those doctrines – while we uproot the superstitions
> of strange worship, let us free ourselves from those creations of
> ignorance.[49]
>
> HAKHAM AVRAHAM PEREIRA MENDES

Unfortunately, history has shown us that the stacks are usually bet against
the *hakhamim* that have tried to clear such dark clouds. Some of our greatest
hakhamim have faced detractors who could only respond to intellectually
broad and honest presentations of Torah with emotions and actions akin to
revulsion, disgust, and even violence.

> They call one to whom God has given the ability to
> understand rational principles... a heretic and non-believer,
> and his books they call external books, because they do not
> have the spirit needed to understand a rational principle.[50]
>
> HAKHAM YITZHAK OF AKKO

> Alas! Let one feel the urge to master some foreign knowledge,
> seeing that it enables him by the added light to discern more
> clearly the true meaning of the Torah itself, and most of his
> contemporaries will not hesitate to ascribe wickedness to his
> conduct.[51]
>
> HAKHAM YA'AKOV ANATOLI

> If you were to mention any of these ideas to the theologians of
> our time, they would be even more angry and repulsed. The
> only cure is to avoid them, for they hate logic and philosophy.[52]
>
> HAKHAM HOTER BEN SHELOMO

---

[49] Avraham Pereira Mendes, *Sermons*, Sermon IV, p. 53

[50] Yitzhak of Akko (Goldreich's quotation, Oxford manuscript 1911, *Me'irat Einayim*, p. 412)

[51] Ya'akov Anatoli, *Malmad haTalmidim*, Introduction

[52] Hoter ben Shelomo, *Siraj al-Uqul* (Available in Tzvi Langermann, *Yemenite Midrash*, p. 272)

As a result, many have abandoned an embrace of the world through the lens of Torah. They are, therefore, lacking a framework, a system, and a context to help them manage the constant chaos of content.

> *Today, text and information reign supreme in all sectors of society… We have a surplus of data and text. What we do not readily have is context… We must offer systems of thought that can be used as a multifaceted lens through which we can assess and evaluate our responses to a world that is developing and changing at lightning speed.*[53]
>
> RABBI JOSEPH DWECK

> *The Torah coordinates and unites the spiritual thoughts of the nation, that is to say, the sciences of the logic, nature, and theology towards the one goal, which is: knowledge of Reality as it is and the knowledge of God and the verification of His unity.*[54]
>
> HAKHAM YITZHAK DAYAN

Many questions emerge out of this deeply unfortunate state of affairs.

Why should we lose a future generation of Torah-true thought and observance that is enhanced through an appreciation for the worldly knowledge around us?

Why must we reduce our birth-right to childish analyses that lack intellectual rigour, depth, and peer-review?

Why have we abandoned principles for details, and relationship for shortcuts?[55]

Are we to ignore the worldly knowledge exhibited by our Talmudic giants?

Are we to forget the intellectual contributions of our Golden Age?

---

[53] Joseph Dweck, *Rupture & Reconstruction: A Sephardic Response*, Tradition 52:3 (2020). This essay is recommended reading.

[54] Yitzhak Dayan, *Minhat Yehuda of Yehuda 'Atiyya*, p. 20

[55] To appreciate this question, read all of Yeshayahu 1.

WORKING DEFINITIONS

The lack of working definitions is a major reason why we are where we are. Working definitions can provide us with practical anchoring points to aid in our understanding of a vision of reality based on Torah, and here are a few.

God is not a celestial dictator that takes pleasure from human obedience; He is Existence itself[56], from which everything is sourced in, and of which nothing but silence suffices when trying to describe Him.

Torah is not primarily a historical presentation, nor a series of fairy-tales exaggerated by *midrashic* misuse; it is God's handiwork written in the language of mankind[57], teeming with principles and lessons of eternal relevance, and serving as a lens through which we view the world.

Prophetic utterances are not magical spells with superficial relevance; they are insights from the outside (*shamayim*), received by an individual at the peak of intellectual and experiential excellence, through the knowledge of Existence and all of His ways (*derakhim*).[58]

Talmudic statements are not irrational and fanciful lessons for the untrained mind; they are *"abstruse ideas, intended only for the elect, that lurk behind a veil of mystery."*[59]

Faith is not simply the blind belief in that which we cannot know, nor is it the excuse to use to avoid action; it is *faithfulness*[60] – the loyalty and commitment required to achieve knowledge of God (*da'at*) and to act upon it, serving as our weapon of war against cognitive dissonance.

---

[56] Rambam, *Thirteen Principles of Faith*, Principle 1; Ramhal, *Derekh HaShem*, Section 1, Chapter 1, Point 3

[57] Yevamot 71a, Bava Metzia 31b

[58] Rambam, *Moreh haNevukhim*, Part 1, Chapter 34

[59] Ya'akov Anatoli, *Malmad haTalmidim*, Matan Torah, p. 119a

[60] Shabbat 31a

Prayer is not a superstitious incantation by our vocal organs, designed solely to disrupt the laws of nature; it is an ego-destructing expression of our primal longing for God, raising us above all other mammals.

Halakha and ritual are not merely rotes of action forced upon us due to the peer pressure of ancestry; they are the physical reinforcements of our most sacred ideas within the context of relationship *(berit)*, serving as powerful touchpoints of love and care to our past, and to our Creator.

Judaism is not a dogmatic religion that serves to institutionalise truth; it is the framework of Jewish life that was formed by the divinely-mandated rabbinic enterprise, in order to maintain a semblance of Torah during life in exile.

My goal in this book is not to add another fancy quotation to the thousands of books that already exist attesting to how influential, relevant, and eternal our weekly Torah portions are. Rather, it is my hope that the *ideas* shared in this book will influence connected and disconnected members of Yisrael alike to broaden their *intellectual* love for Torah, while deepening their *experiential* love for God.

Sina Kahen
London, England
Adar 5780 – March 2020

the context

These matters are well-known, there is almost nothing novel in them. Nonetheless, I saw it fit to write them in a book, because it is the way of the Sepharadi rabbis that their creations in all areas of Jewish thought, their outlook on Judaism in general and about current issues in particular – are unknown. Something terrible is taking place in regard to everything which is connected to the cultural, religious, and educational tradition of the Sepharadi Jews in our times. Things that in the recent past were known to every Rabbinic student, are unknown today even to those who are referred to as "giants of the generation". We, who were raised on the ancient educational tradition which was kept alive for generation after generation in the houses of study of the Sepharadim, see the new state of affairs with a heavy heart and despondent eyes. The bridges with the past have been destroyed, the markers along the road have been uprooted, the pathways have been erased and covered with dirt. What will the young one who wishes to reveal his past, do? Where will he turn? Who will show him the way? *

HAKHAM YOSEF FAUR

The Context

In 1147, the *Sepharadim* (Spanish Jews) were forced to leave Spain as a new form of radical Islam took control of the region. Many of these *Sepharadim* left for *Ashkenazi* lands, such as southern France.[61] This region was to become the latest, and by no means the last, battleground for a recurring cultural, ideological, and mimetic conflict between the *Sepharadim* and the *Ashkenazim*.

The *Sepharadi* arrivals were products of an Andalusian[62] civilisation that was *"dazzling, vibrant, endlessly stimulating"*[63], boasting *"the most sophisticated Jewish community in the world."*[64] Their *hakhamim* had a predilection for a Torah rooted in tradition, rationality, and worldly knowledge – catalysed by the works of homegrown giants and polymaths such as Rabbi Yosef Ibn Migash (Ri Migash), Rabbi Yitzhak Alfasi (Rif), and Rabbi Moshe ben Maimon (Rambam). Contrary to their *Sepharadi* brethren of northern Spain, these *Sepharadim* of southern Spain were not in close proximity to, nor influenced by, *Ashkenazi* modes of thought from neighbouring France and Germany.[65] Indeed, the approach of Andalusian Jewry was deemed to

---

* Jose Faur, *Rabbi Yisrael Moshe Hazzan: The Man and His Works*, Introduction

[61] Specifically, the area of Languedoc (Occitania).

[62] Andalusia was the largest of the ancient divisions of Spain (*Sepharad*), located in the south.

[63] David Berger, *Judaism's Encounter with Other Cultures*, p. 75

[64] Gregg Stern, *Philosophy and Rabbinic Culture*, p. 12

[65] *Sepharadim* of northern Spain (e.g. Catalonia) were influenced by the neighbouring *Ashkenazim* of the Franco-German Rhineland, while the culturally and ideologically distinct *Sepharadim* of southern Spain (Andalusia) were not. For example, the most famous northern *Sepharadim* (Nahmanides and Rashba) introduced *kabbalistic* and *halakhic* doctrines of *Ashkenaz* into Spain. Rashba was a student of Yonah Gerondi (foremost student of the *Ashkenazi* Shelomo ben Montpellier, leader of the movement against the southern *Sepharadi*, Rambam) and Nahmanides (student of Yehuda ben Yakar, Azriel ben Menahem (student of Yitzhak the Blind, amongst whom historical *kabbalah* appeared), and Natan ben Meir – all students of *Ashkenazi* academies). It was in this context that *kabbalah* in Spain developed. See Jose Faur, *The Legal Thinking of the Tosafot; In The Shadow of History; A Crisis of Categories.*

be the continuation of the approach of Babylonian Jewry – the civilisation that produced the Babylonian Talmud.[66]

Their *Ashkenazi* hosts, on the other hand, were living amidst a surrounding Christian culture that was *"primitive, culturally unproductive, and stimulated little more than the instinct for self-preservation."*[67] As a result of their surroundings, this community of French *Ashkenazim* had *"little knowledge of philosophy, but were familiar with the mystical teachings of German pietism, which developed esotericism into a full-fledged and distinct worldview."*[68]

The *Sepharadi* arrivals believed that Torah learning, the worship of God, and the glorification of the Jewish people in the eyes of the nations, are all enriched by worldly knowledge. Thus, this community boasted *hakhamim* and laypeople who branched into cartography, medicine, mathematics, astronomy, philosophy, Hebrew and Arabic philology, and poetry.[69]

> *In the classical Sepharadic tradition, free use of the human*
> *intellect was very much connected with faith, and it ought not*
> *to surprise us to find deep piety alongside critical thinking.*[70]

We can contrast this to their *Ashkenazi* hosts, and even some *Sepharadim* amongst them[71], who were very wary of philosophy and science, deeming them to be diversions from Torah, and a road to heresy.

> *Whoever would enter from the beginning into this science will*
> *never escape from it … he will never grasp the wisdom of the*

---

[66] The legal methodology and cultural disposition of Andalusian Jewry in *Sepharad* (Spain) were not innovations produced wholly within its borders. Rather, they were deemed to be the continuation of the approach of the *hakhamim* who formulated the Talmud in Babylonia (*Geonim*). After being expelled from Babylonia, many Jews settled in Spain and established great Torah centres. See Yevamot 115b; see *Sefer haItim*, p. 267; see *Tarbitz haShana*, p. 396; watch Henry Abramson, *Jewess of Adra*; see Abarbanel, *Commentary to Book of Ovadia*, 1:20: *"Jewish settlers were first exiled to Spain by Nebuhadnezzar after the destruction of the first Temple."*
[67] Marc Angel, *Voices in Exile*, p. 67
[68] Rina Lapidus, *Happiness in Premodern Judaism*, p. 269
[69] See 'Ornament of the World and the Jews of Spain', in *Humanities* magazine (7th December 2019), a publication of the National Endowment for the Humanities.
[70] Andrew Gluck, *Keter Malkhut of Shelomo Ibn Gabirol*, Preface xii
[71] See footnote 65.

> Law [halakha], which is the paths of life, since his heart will
> always be with natural science ... these sciences and the Law
> are mutually exclusive and are not compatible with one
> another.[72]

> There is reason to fear that the philosophically inspired
> youths, who have not yet seen the light of Torah, will turn the
> whole country to heresy.[73]

For four to five generations after the arrival of *Sepharadim*, the Jewish culture
of southern France had become transformed into one which embraced
philosophy and science, with many of its most famous Jewish scholars
embodying the classical *Sepharadi* approach.

> There are many scholars of southern France who are
> completely familiar with the science of the Talmud – being its
> perpetual students, contributing new insights and
> interpretations – and in addition, are experts in the sciences,
> whether all of them, most of them, or some of them.[74]

However, this development was not to continue unchallenged. The pietistic
doctrines from neighbouring Germany (*Ashkenaz*) – filled with
demonology and asceticism[75] – were publicly spread in southern France.
The bearers of these *kabbalistic* doctrines could not suffer in silence over the
Sepharadi claim that philosophy and science could aid in the study of Torah
and in the service of God.

---

[72] Asher ben Yehiel, *Responsa of Rosh*, 55:9

[73] Crescas Vidal's letter to Rashba, in Abba Mari, *Minhat Qena'ot*, p. 372. This is referenced in Gregg Stern, *Philosophy and Rabbinic Culture*, p. 157

[74] Menaghem Meiri, *Bet haBehirah*, Introduction, Avot, p. 143. This is referenced in Gregg Stern, *Philosophy and Rabbinic Culture*, p. 28

[75] Many of these *kabbalistic* doctrines of *Ashkenaz* seemed to evoke the Gnostic Christian and neo-Platonic doctrines that were popular in the lands of *Ashkenaz* at the time. For a thorough analysis of this topic, see Joseph Dan & Karl Grozinger, *Mysticism, Magic, and Kabbalah in Ashkenazi Judaism*; Gershom Scholem, *The Origins of Kabbalah*; and (especially) Jose Faur, *A Crisis of Categories: Kabbalah and the Rise of Apostasy in Spain*.

At the risk of gross oversimplification, this clash was simply the latest episode in a controversy that *still* debates the marriage between Torah and worldly knowledge; the difference between *isolation* and *integration*.

This controversy would repeatedly erupt throughout Jewish history, and result in public bans instituted by *isolationists* who were against such a marriage, and counter-bans were elicited by *integrationists* who defended it.[76]

Throughout the generations, those *hakhamim* against integration included Rabbi Shelomo of Montpellier, Rabbi Shelomo ben Aderet (Rashba), Rabbi Asher ben Yehiel (Rosh), and others.[77] Some of the bans led to prominent books written by Jewish philosophers to be destroyed and burned.

> *[We shall excommunicate] any member of the community who, being under the age of 25 years, shall study the works of the Greeks on natural science or metaphysics, whether in the original language or in translation.*[78]

> *For the sons have been exiled from their fathers' tables; they have defiled themselves with the food of the gentiles and the wine of their feasts. They have mixed with them and become used to their deeds … courtiers have been permitted to study Greek wisdom, to become acquainted with medicine, to learn mathematics and geometry, other knowledge and tricks, so that they make a living in royal courts and palaces.*[79]

> *These [philosophical] books, since they are of Jewish authorship, if some of them turn toward heretical ideas – even if this is only hinted at in the most obscure fashion – it is an*

---

[76] For a thorough analysis of this history, see Jose Faur, *Anti-Maimonidean Demons*. Available online at: http://moreshetsepharad.org/media/Anti-Maimonidean_Demons.pdf

[77] In varying degrees, as some of these *hakhamim* were open to some worldly knowledge.

[78] Shelomo ben Aderet, *Responsa of Rashba*, pt. 1, no. 415. This is referenced in Gregg Stern, *Philosophy and Rabbinic Culture*, p. 195

[79] Nahmanides, referenced in Ben-Sasson and Haim Hillel, *Maimonidean Controversy*, Volume 13, p. 371-381. However, Nahmanides took a nuanced approach in the debate.

> *obligation to perform upon them the positive commandment:*
> *destroy, burn, obliterate.*[80]

Those who followed the predominantly *Sepharadi* school of thought never took to such bans and statements lightly. These were direct attacks upon their knowledge of God, and upon their cherished tradition *(mesorah)* of integration.

The *hakhamim* on the integrationist side of this historical debate have notably included Rambam, Rabbi Menahem Meiri (The Meiri), Rabbi David Kimhe (Radak), and others. The integrationist side responded to the bans and statements against the study of philosophy and the sciences with their own counter-bans and counter-statements, wishing to …

> *… excommunicate the promulgators of the original ban, and their allies, and to excommunicate anyone who prevents his son from studying physics or metaphysics or Gentile sciences.*[81]

> *Please look into the mighty pattern of the benefits of philosophy to all of us … thanks to [the Sages'] familiarity with the Arabic language, they had the great opportunity to smell the perfume of the sciences. It is thanks to this that they began to elaborate and clarify many of their opinions on the Torah. Relinquish your ban, for the heart of this people will not turn away from philosophy and its books as long as there is breath in their frame and soul in their bodies, especially as together with it, they are true to Torah and commandments.*[82]

---

[80] Abba Mari, *Minhat Qena'ot*, p. 575. This is referenced in Gregg Stern, *Philosophy and Rabbinic Culture*, p. 142.

[81] This ban, formulated by the *hakhamim* of Montpellier in defence of worldly knowledge, was ratified by local royal officials. Referenced in Marc Saperstein, *The Conflict over the Rashba's Herem on Philosophical Study,* Jewish History 1:2: 37, n.19. For the text of the counter-ban, see Kaufmann, *Deux letters,* p. 222

[82] Jedaiah ben Avraham Beresi, referenced in Ben-Sasson and Haim Hillel, *Maimonidean Controversy,* Volume 13, p. 371-381

It is widely known among our people that our Sages instructed
and warned us to learn the wisdom concerning the unity of
God [philosophy], as well as external forms of wisdom that
will enable us to answer heretics and know the matters utilised
by them to destroy our Torah. [They] also instructed us to
study astrology and the vanities of idol-worship, [which] one
cannot learn from the Torah or the Talmud. Moreover, they
ruled that no one can be appointed to the Sanhedrin to decide
the law unless he knows these disciplines, and medicine.[83]

In its latest manifestation, the fire of the controversy was alive in southern
France. Both camps held firm to their convictions.

One camp's "heresy" is the other camp's "Torah Truth." One
camp sees itself as upholding the honour of the Torah, while
the other camp views the former as displaying tremendous
ignorance and shaming the Torah in the process, if not
worse.[84]

Nevertheless, the integrationists came out victorious in this particular battle.
The efforts to expunge worldly knowledge from the realm of Torah learning
proved ineffective in southern France. The leading authority of the region
was The Meiri – an integrationist – and he had the last word on the matter.

[Foreign] learning is no longer foreign material that might be
banned; it is part of Jewish culture. There are Jewish tracts on
the sciences, and the sciences have been incorporated into non-
philosophic works as well. The sciences are necessary ... The
religious problems raised by philosophic study are
inconsiderable in relation to its benefits. Our distinguished
specialists in the sciences should be allowed to pursue their
work unhindered, and their writings – however troubling –
should not be suspected of heresy. To restrict access to the

---

[83] Radak, *Qovez Teshubot haRambam 3*, p. 5b
[84] Howard Kreisel, *The Torah Commentary of Rabbi Nissim ben Moshe of Marseilles*

sciences – even from a few people for a short time – would almost certainly be to their detriment and the detriment of our community. Experience has shown that excommunications do no good. Let us put them all away, and allow each group within southern France to act as it sees fit.[85]

Over the course of Jewish history, however, both sides have failed in convincing each other, and no resolution has been reached. However, with the region's impending plagues, massacres, anti-rationalism – coupled with a lack of *Sepharadi* educational centres, and a standardisation of Jewish thought and practice – the classic *Sepharadi* approach began to wane.[86] Indeed, the major uprooting of Spanish Jewry in 1492 was a watershed moment for classical *Sepharad*, both physically and ideologically.[87]

The century following the expulsion of the Jews from Spain was a period of intellectual and spiritual creativity among the Sepharadim. While rationalism and philosophical inquiry were ardently defended by some thinkers, the growing tendency was against philosophy and in favour of kabbalah.[88]

The Jews of Spain in the past prospered and were the crown and garland of all the Jewish diaspora. Now our best and wisest children have left us. Nothing remains of our science. At

---

[85] Menahem Meiri's letter to Abba Mari, in Simeon ben Joseph, *Hoshen Mishpat*. This is summarised and referenced in Gregg Stern, *Philosophy and Rabbinic Culture*, p. 210

[86] For an analysis of many of these unfortunate developments, see Zvi Zohar, *Rabbinic Creativity in the Modern Middle East*; and Joseph Dweck, *Rupture & Reconstruction: A Sephardic Response*, Tradition 52:3 (2020)

[87] Pre-expulsion *Sepharad* had hosted two of the most influential traditions within Judaism: the *rational*-intellectual tradition (in the southern regions), and the *mystical*-intellectual tradition (in the northern regions, influenced by neighbouring *Ashkenaz*). However, Talmudic mysticism is different to the *kabbalah* of pre-expulsion Spanish Jewry, which is different to the popularised Lurianic *kabbalah* of post-expulsion Jewry. For more analysis, watch Daniel Bouskila, *From Spain to Safed: The Sephardic Roots of Kabbalah*, available from The Sephardic Jewish Brotherhood of America. For the differences between Talmudic mysticism and contemporary Jewish mysticism, watch Aaron Haleva, *The Foundations of Rabbinic Mysticism*, available from The Sephardic Jewish Brotherhood of America.

[88] Marc Angel, *Voices in Exile*, p. 68

> *the river-bed whose waters once carried ships, there cannot be found today even small brooks. Our science has thus vanished.*[89]

> *There are many Sephardic Jews who have completely embraced the new milieu established by the Ashkenazic world and, having been fully educated in Ashkenazic yeshivot and schools, many Sephardim in America, Israel, and Europe have come to know the Ashkenazic way as the only way. We have espoused their norms of dress and their mode of religious thought and practice. The traditional way of Sephardic Orthodox life is becoming something of an endangered species.*[90]

However, this classic *Sepharadi* tradition continued to produce remarkable *hakhamim* to this very day, whose works have continued to resonate with each passing generation. Further, the *Sepharadi* approach of integration managed to take hold beyond the borders of Babylonia, Spain, and southern France – most notably in the Yemen and Italy.

> *Of all the Jewish communities, it seems that only in that of the Yemen did the dual commitment to philosophical inquiry and to religious practice as codified in the rabbinic tradition establish itself as the norm for a lengthy period.*[91]

> *Italy's Jewish intellectuals created a unique and enduring synthesis of the great literary and philosophical heritage of the Andalusian Jews.*[92]

With the grace of God, coupled with the pressing needs of our intellectually advanced era, we are witnessing this classic *Sepharadi* school of thought

---

[89] Moses Aragel, *Biblia de la Casa de Alba*, p. 13. This is referenced in Jose Faur, *In the Shadow of History*, p. 9

[90] Joseph Dweck, *Rupture & Reconstruction: A Sephardic Response*, Tradition 52:3 (2020). This essay is recommended reading.

[91] Yitzhak Tzvi Langermann, *Yemenite Midrash*, Introduction

[92] Alessandro Guetta, *Italian Jewry in the Early Modern Era*, Blurb/Book Description

move from the side-lines to take centre stage again, as a vital approach to Torah and Jewish life.

The popular re-emergence of this *Sepharadi* approach is not tradition-driven, nostalgia-driven, nor is it rooted in post-modern or new-age thinking. Rather, its reappearance is reality-driven – a revitalisation of a legal (*halakhic*) and ideological (*hashkafic*) tradition that is equipped to constantly monitor and respond to each and every element of a developing world, through the tried-and-tested lens of our divine and eternal Torah.

Unfortunately, many within the Jewish world today are totally unaware of this classical *Sepharadi* approach, even though it played such an influential role in Jewish history that it has since been dubbed 'The Golden Age'.[93] Indeed, the many Jewish communities today that pride themselves on embracing worldly knowledge are no doubt the ideological descendants of this *Sepharadi* – and ultimately, Talmudic[94] – school of thought.

In its latest manifestations today, this *Sepharadi* approach does not find itself tethered to any particular geography, nor to any side of the *Sepharadi/Ashkenazi* racial divide. Ironically, many of the greatest proponents of this school of thought have since been *Ashkenazim*, while many *Sepharadim* (eastern/*mizrahi*) have adopted the opposite worldview as their own. The western *Sepharadim*, however, have not forgotten their tradition.

I hope that it will soon become clear to the reader that the **ideas** found within this series find their roots deeply entrenched in the nourishing soil of this rejuvenating, esteemed, and original *Sepharadi* tradition of integration.

> *From the rising of the sun to its setting, from north to south, there was never such a chosen people as the Jews of Spain, in beauty and pleasantness; and afterwards, there will never be another such people.*[95]

---

[93] For a thorough analysis, see Maria Rosa Menocal, *The Ornament of The World*
[94] See footnote 66.
[95] Abarbanel, *Mayanei haYeshua*, Introduction

bereshit

בראשית

Bereshit – The Primacy of Speech

Bereshit represents the earliest stories of our species.

Before we are introduced to Adam and Hava – the archetypes of Homo sapiens on earth – we immediately notice the creative role that *speech* plays in the process of Creation itself.

From when *"God began to create heaven and earth" (1:1)* to the point at which *"the heaven and the earth were completed" (2:1)*, the faculty of speech is referred to numerous times.

> God said... (1:3, 6, 9, 11, 14, 20, 24, 26, 28, 29)

In *Bereshit*, the original template of reality is being formed from *divine* commands of speech.

> *The world was created with ten utterances.*[1]
>
> PIRKEI AVOT

Ever since then, the subsequent development of new realities upon that original template have been formed from *human* commands of speech – producing civilisations, technological innovations, and mammalian domination.

> *Speech shaped the world as it is today. The emergence of the spoken word facilitated the largest feats of collective endeavor, allowing us to dominate the world.*[2]
>
> TREVOR COX

> *The human capacity for language has played a critical role in the development of civilizations, the transmission of knowledge, and our ability to collectively shape our environments.*[3]
>
> THE SCIENTIFIC AMERICAN

Speech has allowed Homo sapiens to transform the intangible into the tangible. This is even visible at the molecular level, as tangible changes occur to the brain structure of someone who has listened to the intangible spoken word of another.

> *Speech is the root of creation; it converts the abstract potential*
> *of thought into the reality of a practical existence.*[4]
> RABBI AKIVA TATZ

Speech brings language to life, allowing us to create meaning through a system of symbolic communication. This unique ability to speak is a major reason why Homo sapiens survived, and Neanderthals did not. While other mammals have been able to communicate at a very basic level, none have the speaking capabilities of modern man.

The Torah is forthright in emphasising this fundamental and unique distinction from the outset.

> *The man became a living being. (2:7)*

The popular English translations of this line use the words *"living* being", as quoted above. Yet, it is the *Targum Onkelos* – the ancient translation of the Torah – that translates the words as *"speaking* being". According to this ancient translation, the determinant feature of this new living being on earth – Homo sapiens – is its capacity to *speak.*

However, we know that the vocal anatomies of other mammals are perfectly capable of creating words. The rapid rhythms of mammalian calls can precisely match that of a human. So, what did Homo sapiens *(adam)* possess that other mammals did not?

Intelligence.

> *"And God created man in His image, in the image of God He*
> *created him." (1:27)*
>> *– The 'image of God' refers to:*
>> *intellectual perception.*[5] (RAMBAM)
>> *intellectual achievement.*[6] (BAHYA BEN ASHER)

> *the human intellect.*[7] (SEFORNO)
> *the power to comprehend and to discern.*[8] (RASHI)
> *rationality.*[9] (HAKHAM HOTER BEN SHELOMO)

The Torah informs us that man was created in the image of God, and that this likeness refers specifically to the human intellect – the unique tool we use as we wander the earth.

> *The intellect is God and God is the intellect. This is why Moshe was called "a man of God", because God was always in his mind.*[10]
>
> YOSEF IBN KASPI

> *We are not directed to conquer the earth with muscular power, but to subdue it by means of man's superior intellect. It means that man is to use his intelligence to prevent predators from invading his habitats, demonstrating the fact that man is superior by outwitting the beasts.*[11]
>
> SEFORNO

> *Our intelligence has enabled us to overcome the restrictions of our biological heritage and to change ourselves in the process. We are the only species that does this.*[12]
>
> RAY KURZWEIL

Indeed, our ability to speak is directly linked to our intellectual and reasoning capabilities.

> *There is no speech without reason, and no reason without speech.*[13]
>
> MAX MULLER

> *Something happened when Homo sapiens came into existence… an improvement in cognitive ability… led to a virtuous cycle, whereby more sophisticated language allowed more complex thought, and this allowed modern humans to out-think and out-compete Neanderthals.*[14]
>
> TREVOR COX

Speech is therefore the product of a cognitive revolution that also gave Homo sapiens the ability to reason, to reflect, to create.

> *Intelligence is not only the ability to reason; it is also the ability to find relevant material in memory and to deploy attention when needed.*[15]
>
> DANIEL KAHNEMANN

> *Intelligence fosters creative achievement.*[16]
>
> EMANUAL JAUK

This cognitive capacity is the powerhouse that allows man to contextualise basic symbols (letters) and turn them into complex communication (speech). It is truly astonishing to note that the Hebrew alphabet contains no vowels – the crucial unit that aids in the pronunciation and sense of words. Therefore, when man is presented with a random arrangement of Hebrew letters, he must rely upon his unique cognitive capacity to make sense of them.

Yisrael is taught to view this cognitive revolution as the most exemplar representation of the divine within each of us. All the while, today's ideological proponents of nihilism struggle to explain the appearance of this defining transformation.

> *The cognitive revolution ... what caused it? We are not sure.*[17]
>
> YUVAL NOAH HARARI

It is befitting of our most primal story to begin with an affirmation that our most uniquely human feature – the intellect – is that which we share in likeness with God.

To utilise and develop this exceptional feature of our primordial software is to express, to recognise, and to be under the providence of, divinity itself.

> *You must know that the ultimate human achievement is attained in the most honourable human power – reason.*[18]
>
> AVRAHAM IBN MIGASH

Intelligence is the basis of the Torah. The Torah was not given to ignoramuses. Man's intelligence is the angel which mediates between him and his God.[19]

AVRAHAM IBN EZRA

I believe that [divine] providence is consequent upon the intellect and attached to it.[20]

RAMBAM

Truly, in all stages of life, if we seek permanent peace for our souls, we shall direct our steps towards God with our reasoning faculties at the frontline.[21]

HAKHAM YA'AKOV ANATOLI

Conversely, to abandon our intellect in exchange for an irrational and caricaturist vision of reality is to lose our human status and to devolve into lower mammalian being.

The intellect represents the evolutionary distinction between pre-Homo sapiens and Homo sapiens; between pre-Adam and Adam.

You must know that whoever does not possess [intellect] is not a human, but an animal merely having the shape and configuration of a human.[22]

RAMBAM

What distinguishes man from all other creatures? Is it not his power of thought, his searching mind?[23]

HAKHAM YA'AKOV ANATOLI

Intellect is the dividing line between man and beast.[24]

SHELOMO IBN GABIROL

For we are of the genus of the animals, similar in genus to the lowest of the creeping insects. We are also their equal in every respect, unless we realize the potential of our intellect.[25]

YOSEF IBN KASPI

We should not neglect to know the nature of that which makes us intelligent beings, or else we don't deserve to be regarded

> *intelligent or even human beings, but instead are likened to*
> *cattle and beast.*[26]
>
> HAKHAM HILLEL OF VERONA

> *The rational mind is the distinctive human feature.*[27]
>
> RAMHAL

> *He, who will not reason, is a bigot;*
> *He, who cannot reason, is a fool;*
> *He, who dares not reason, is a slave.*[28]
>
> WILLIAM DRUMMOND

And yet, we must remain humbly aware of the limits of intellect and reason. After all, experiential tools such as spirituality, faith, and imagination are required to maintain the balance of being.

So what are we to do with rationality when our very own existence surpasses rational explanation?

We are to remember the following principle: that which stretches beyond the limits of reason does not negate that which resides within those very limits. The unknowable (*shemayim*) should never lead us to abandon our most divine feature, for a descent into an irrationality that is fed by the unfortunate, yet comforting, product of anti-intellect – superstition.

Supra-rational phenomena are beyond our understanding, not beneath it.[29]

Indeed, the Torah itself is beyond rationality, not against it.

> *The Torah does not contradict rationality: it transcends it.*
> *Beyond the cutting edge of reason lies a higher reality that*
> *rational humanity can intuitively grasp but cannot*
> *articulate.*[30]
>
> HAKHAM YOSEF FAUR

References

1. Pirkei Avot, 5:1
2. Trevor Cox, *Now You're Talking*, Introduction
3. Viorica Marian and Sayaru Hayakawa, *How Language Shapes the Brain*, Scientific American
4. Akiva Tatz, *As Dawn Meets the Night*, p.109
5. Rambam, *Mishneh Torah*, Hilkhot Yesodei haTorah, 4:8
6. Bahya ben Asher, Commentary on Bereshit 1:27
7. Seforno, Commentary Bereshit 1:27
8. Rashi, Commentary on Bereshit 1:27
9. Hoter ben Shelomo, *Siraj al-Uqul*, Bereshit 1:26 (Available in Tzvi Langermann, *Yemenite Midrash*, p. 232)
10. Yosef Ibn Kaspi, *Maskiyot Kesef*, p. 98
11. Seforno, Commentary on Bereshit 1:28
12. Ray Kurzweil, *How to Create a Mind*, Introduction
13. Ludwig Noire, *The Origin and Philosophy of Language*, p. 73
14. Trevor Cox, *Now You're Talking*, Introduction
15. Daniel Kahnemann, *Thinking Fast & Slow*, Chapter 3
16. Emanual Jauk, *The relationship between intelligence and creativity*, Intelligence. p. 212-221
17. Yuval Noah Harari, *Sapiens*, Chapter 2
18. Avraham Ibn Migash, *Kevod Elohim*, Chapter 24, p. 51b
19. Avraham Ibn Ezra, Introduction to Bereshit, p. 10
20. Rambam, *Moreh haNevukhim*, 3:17
21. Ya'akov Anatoli, *Malmad haTalmidim*, Behaalotecha, p. 130b
22. Rambam, *Moreh haNevukhim*, 1:7
23. Ya'akov Anatoli, *Malmad haTalmidim*, Terumah, p. 73b
24. Shelomo Ibn Gabirol, *Choice of Pearls*
25. Yosef Ibn Kaspi, *Adnei Kesef*, p.151
26. Hillel of Verona, *Tagmule haNefesh*, Introduction
27. Ramhal, *Mesillat Yesharim*, Chapter 22
28. William Drummond, *Academical Questions*, Preface
29. Supra-rationality is defined as that which transcends rationality and is incomprehensible by human reason alone. This should *never* be equated with irrationality (the quality of being illogical or unreasonable). For further analysis, read the *Introduction* of this book.
30. Jose Faur, *Homo Mysticus*, p. 109

noah

נח

Noah – *Context Matters*

The perversity and corruption of Noah's generation knew no bounds.

> *The members of Noah's generation sinned increasingly, and*
> *so were punished increasingly.*[1]
>
> TALMUD BAVLI

> *The urge to do good had succumbed to the urge to do evil,*
> *completely.*[2]
>
> RADAK

Water, an element historically associated with purification[3], appears in this *perashah* in a form that equally had no bounds – a flood. This flood is the instrument that God uses to destroy the depravity that had usurped life on earth.

Due to his righteousness, Noah is given a flood warning from God that he responds to with faithfulness *(emunah)*, ultimately saving himself and his family. This warning is coupled with the divine demand for the first known example of human innovation: the construction of a great ark, for protection from the flood.

It is only after this purification that God promises to never again destroy the world with a flood. The symbol of this assurance is a rainbow.

> *And God said "This is the sign of the covenant that I set*
> *between Me and you and every living creature that is with you,*
> *for everlasting generations: My rainbow I have set in the*
> *clouds to be a sign of the covenant. (9:13)*

Does this imply that the rainbow was a new phenomenon, appearing for the first time since Creation? Had it not existed *before* the flood?

Some of our *hakhamim* held as such[4], claiming that this was indeed the first time that a rainbow had graced the skies. However, this view is problematic considering the discoveries of scientific inquiry: we know that rainbows occur naturally when light is refracted through water.

> *The reflection of a rainbow is from very small particles continuous with one another, and in this case the particles are fully formed water. We get a rainbow, too, if a man sprinkles fine drops in a room turned to the sun so that the sun is shining in part of the room and throwing a shadow in the rest.*[5]
>
> ARISTOTLE

Rainbows, therefore, have existed for as long as light and water have existed, which *predate* the flood. Given this scientific reality, can we really take this verse at surface level and claim that no rainbows existed until *after* the flood?

Ramban (Nahmanides) offers a solution that recognises the impossibility of such a contradiction.

> *As for us, we have no choice but to accept the opinion of the Greeks who maintain that the rainbow is an entirely natural phenomenon caused by the sun's rays striking the moist air after a rainfall. The term "My rainbow" implies that it had existed earlier. Therefore, we explain the verses to mean that the rainbow is from the time of Creation.*[6]
>
> RAMBAN

Ramban states that he has *"no choice"* but to accept the scientists of his time (the Greeks), and he therefore accepts that the rainbow's appearance after the flood could not have been new. Nevertheless, the *context* of this rainbow definitely was new: after the flood, the rainbow was to now serve as the sign of relationship – a shared covenant (*berit*) between God and human civilisation. A key component of this eternal relationship is free will – the unique ability of man to choose between viability or catastrophe.

> *The covenant of Noah is a covenant of fate. God says: "Never again will I destroy the world, but I cannot promise that you*

> *will never destroy the world, because I have given you free will.*
> *All I can do is teach you how not to destroy the world.'[7]*
>
> RABBI JONATHAN SACKS

What is most astonishing about Ramban's commentary, however, is that he sees no issue with re-examining the literal reading of the Torah *(peshat)* when established proof clearly contradicts it, even if such proof comes from outside the tradition. After all,

> *One should accept the truth, regardless of its source.[8]*
>
> RAMBAM

In recent times, many are unaware of this classical tradition of viewing Torah and reality as integrated partners, and not as separate, conflicting worlds. The proponents of this school of thought, and their exegetical methods, are well established.

> *Those passages in the Torah, which in their literal reading (peshat) contain statements that can be refuted by proof, can and must be interpreted otherwise.[9]*
>
> RAMBAM

> *It is a well-known fact that every statement in the Torah is to be understood in its literal reading (peshat) except... for example, if it is rejected by the observation of the senses... or if the literal reading is negated by reason.[10]*
>
> SA'ADIA GAON

> *If there appears something in the Torah which seems to contradict reason or to refute the evidence of our senses then here one should seek for the solution in a figurative interpretation. Reason is the foundation of everything.[11]*
>
> AVRAHAM IBN EZRA

The reason why *reason* is important in unravelling the Torah is due to its clearly divine nature. After all, the Torah could not possibly require us to abandon our intellect – that which is the image of God within us *(tzelem Elohim)*, and that which hosts our very ability to reason?

> *Our divine Torah would never oblige us to believe things which contradict each other or the evidence of our senses. If our religion required us to believe such things, we would reject the religion. For even if it were assumed to be true that we were so required, no divine punishment could follow our refusal to believe such things, since our intellect, with its nature as constituted by God, would not allow us to accept or to believe them but would constantly inform us of their opposite.*[12]
>
> HAKHAM ELIA DEL MEDIGO

It is no wonder that *Truth* – whose pursuit is so powerfully aided by the use of our intellect – is repeatedly presented as being interchangeable with *Torah, prophecy,* and *God.*

> *The signature of God is Truth.*[13]
>
> *Moshe and his Torah are Truth.*[14]
>
> TALMUD BAVLI

> *For Truth, reinforced by God Himself, whose very name is Truth, need never boggle or tremble even when great multitudes are arrayed against it.*[15]
>
> HAKHAM YA'AKOV ANATOLI

Therefore, once we acknowledge the divine hand behind all truths, we can begin to appreciate that *Torah* and *reality* share the same author. If we truly spend some time pondering this fundamental yet forgotten principle, we can only conclude that there can never truly be any conflict between the *word* of God and the *world* of God. If we ever perceive there to be such a thing, it is as a result of our own misunderstanding.

> *Understanding God's world helps us understand God's world.*[16]
>
> RABBI JONATHAN SACKS

> *There is no contradiction whatsoever between the Torah and any of the world's scientific knowledge.*[17]
>
> RABBI AVRAHAM YITZHAK KOOK

References

1. Sanhedrin 108a
2. Radak, Commentary on Bereshit 6:5
3. In both Israelite and Jewish history, water figures in various purification rituals: the ordination of the priests (Shemot 29:4), the sacrifices (Vayikra 1:9), the cure of skin diseases (Vayikra 13:6), bodily emissions (Vayikra 15:5), purification after contact with dead animal carcasses and human corpses (Vayikra 11:24-40, Bamidbar 19:7), the casting away of sins (Micah 7:18-20). Water is perceived as having the ability to wipe impurities clean and allow the person to be recreated or returned.
4. Abarbanel (Commentary on Noah, Chapter 8, Question 15); Ibn Ezra (Commentary on Bereshit, 9:13-14)
5. Aristotle, *Meteorology*, Book 3, Part 4
6. Ramban Bereshit 9:12-17. The opinion that the rainbow predates the Flood is shared by Sa'adia Gaon, Radak, Ran, Yitzhak Caro (Commentaries to Bereshit 9:13), Yitzhak ben Moshe Arama (*Akedat Yitzhak*, Noah, Sha'ar 14), Eliezer Ashkenazi (Ma'asei Hashem, *Ma'aseh Bereshit*, Chapter 28)
7. Jonathan Sacks, *Speech at Lambeth Conference 2008*. Available online: http://www.chiefrabbi.org/UploadedFiles/Articals/lambethconferenc e28july08.pdf
8. Rambam, *Shemoneh Perakim*, Introduction
9. Rambam, *Moreh haNevukhim*, 2 25:2
10. Sa'adia Gaon, *Emunot VeDe'ot*, Book VII
11. Avraham Ibn Ezra, *Sefer haYashar*, Introduction
12. Elia Del Medigo, *Behinat haDat*, Part I, Section 4, p. 81
13. Yoma 69b
14. Sanhedrin 110a
15. Ya'akov Anatoli, *Malmad haTalmidim*, Va'ethanan, p. 157b
16. Jonathan Sacks, *Covenant & Conversation*, Noah 5780
17. Avraham Yitzhak Kook, *Letters of Rav Kook*, Letter 91

lech-lecha

לֶךְ לְךָ

Lech-Lecha – Existential Dynamics

The *perashah* begins with the earliest recorded mandate for human self-discovery.

> *And the Lord said to Avram, "Go for yourself from your land and your birthplace and your father's house to the land that I will show you…" (12:1-2)*

Avram (soon-to-*become* Avraham) is ultimately commanded to discover who he really is – a journey into the unknown. The recognition and receipt of this divine demand was not merely a call from the sky. Rather, Avram (soon-to-*become* Avraham) had to *prepare* himself for enlightenment.

> *Avraham was prepared to behold visions of the Divine Presence.*[1]
>
> KLI YAKAR

> *Rambam maintains that "knowing God", which constitutes the personal goal of the religious life, can only be the culmination of a sober, painstaking, and therefore necessarily lengthy process. Avraham is the prime example of the successful realisation of this goal.*[2]
>
> TZVI LANGERMANN

Why was it that Avraham had to prepare, and what was it that aided in his preparation?

The background setting of *Lech-Lecha* may provide some clues.

An analysis of the cultural backdrop alerts us to a recurring episode of our perennial problem: the human tendency to descend into the depravity of that primal sickness of thought and action – idolatry. This irrationality was prevalent in Avraham's time and place, and it was the generational product of the well-intentioned, but deeply ignorant, descendant of Noah – Enosh.

> *In the days of Enosh, mankind made a big mistake; they said "since God created the stars and spheres in order to run the world, and set them in the heavens and gave them honour; and since they serve God, it is fitting that we praise and glorify them and give them honour also."*
>
> *After this thought took root in their hearts, they began to build temples to the stars and spheres… offer them sacrifices, and bow down to the stars and spheres, out of the false belief that they were thereby fulfilling the desire of the Creator.*[3]
>
> RAMBAM

Contrary to popular belief, monotheism did not evolve out of polytheism; the opposite is true. The belief in a single and all-encompassing deity predates Torah. Therefore, the generation of Enosh thought that the way to express their passion towards this single and non-physical deity was to revere and serve His physical creations, such as the sun, spheres, and other natural entities. As such, passionate paganism benignly grew out of a mistaken understanding of God, ultimately leading to a mistaken method of worship.

Indeed, even Yisrael have occasionally suffered from this erroneous channelling of religious zeal.

> *Rav Ashi said to Menashe, King of Judea: "Since you were so wise, what is the reason you engaged in idol worship?"*
>
> *Menashe, King of Judea, replied: "Had you been there at that time, you would have taken and lifted the hem of your cloak and run after me, [due to the fierce desire to engage in idol worship, and due to the fact that it was a common faith!]"*[4]
>
> TALMUD BAVLI

> *One drive of great passion in us has long been the desire to worship a deity. It was so powerful a drive that it took the nation of Yisrael over one thousand years to find some level of peace with it in their struggles. From the earliest days, our people fought to focus their religious ardour towards God alone. It instead found outlet in all manner of expression and action.*[5]
>
> RABBI JOSEPH DWECK

Avraham, the archetype of kindness, was born into an unkind environment that embraced this antithesis of reality.

> *For in the world of Avraham, all around him, country and nation had become idols whom the individual served and whose glory and greatness were the highest aim in life.*[6]
>
> RABBI SHIMSHON RAPHAEL HIRSCH

It was Avraham's ultimate discovery of self, along with his restlessness with the conventional falsehoods of his time, that led him to critical and philosophical deliberations about the world around him.

> *From the time that the great man [Avraham] was weaned, he began to wonder, thinking to himself, "How is it possible that this sphere should be in continuous motion, without anyone moving or guiding it?" He knew that there is One God, and that He guides the spheres and created everything, and that there is no God besides him.*[7]
>
> RAMBAM

The mission of Avraham was a daring and dangerous mission, but one which would ultimately prove worthwhile.

> *Avraham braved personal danger and abuse in proclaiming religious truth to his generation.*[8]
>
> HAKHAM YA'AKOV ANATOLI

> *Avraham began the most significant project in the history of the world, essentially on his own.*[9]
>
> RABBI AKIVA TATZ

By shattering – quite literally[10] – the anti-scientific and superstitious illusions around him, Avraham experienced rational illumination. He proceeded to analyse the world around him (the effects), to arrive at the discovery of the First Cause, the Source of all Existence – what we call *God*.

> *Man's intellectual research proceeds from the effect to the cause.*[11]
>
> HAKHAM YITZHAK ARAMA

55

As a result of sharing his new-old[12] discoveries, Avraham was able to gather and teach followers who would end up following him throughout his journey to the land in which he and his offspring were to acquire – Canaan.

It is important to note that the shared loyalty of his group of followers could have been based only on *philosophical* principles – the majority of our laws, rituals, and commandments today were not yet revealed by God, after all.

> *The patriarchs [Avraham, Yitzhak, Ya'akov], as well as Noah and Adam, obviously did not observe the Torah laws.*[13]
>
> RAMBAM

> *"Avraham our father fulfilled the entire Torah." (Yoma 28b)
> – This certainly does not mean that he kept the laws as they are today. This would be an impossibility, for most of the Torah's commandments are dependent upon the Exodus from Egypt. Rather, the explanation is that he kept 'the light' of the commandments.*[14]
>
> SHEM MISHMUEL

A famine in the land subsequently forced Avraham's followers to travel south into Egypt, to suffer from demeaning slavery there, and experience relentless assaults to their sense of identity. Philosophical principles – alone – did not seem to suffice.

> *Time wore on, and Yisrael in Egypt learned from the ways of their neighbours and began to worship idols like them; all except for the Tribe of Levi[15], who held fast to the ways of their ancestors, and never worshipped idols. The principle that Avraham had implanted was uprooted and the descendants of Ya'akov went back to making the same mistakes as everyone else.*[16]
>
> RAMBAM

> *Yisrael gradually lost their early faith in the land of their oppressors, forgetting daily more and more the religious teaching of their fathers, and advancing meanwhile in the degraded doctrines of Egyptian theology.*[17]
>
> HAKHAM AVRAHAM PEREIRA MENDES

It is clear that Avraham's philosophical revolution did not automatically provide the tools necessary for a maturing people to survive changing and challenging circumstances. The people required a system of action.

The laws, rituals, and commandments that we practice today are not only the loving means through which we engage in service *(avodah)*, but they are simultaneously the actions that reinforce our most sacred ideas. They are the physical manifestations of our people's philosophy, and without them we are prone to losing sense of our core principles.

> *You know from what I have said that opinions do not last unless they are accompanied by actions that strengthen them, that make them generally known, and that perpetuate them among the multitudes.*[18]
>
> RAMBAM

Philosophy provides *context* to *content* such as law *(halakha)*. It is not merely an intellectually-pleasing exercise, nor is it for waverers. Philosophy is integral to Torah, to acquiring knowledge *(da'at)* of God, and even to enhancing the stature of Yisrael in the eyes of other nations.

> *It is a great honour for our nation when the men among us are perfect in philosophy ... so that other nations might say "surely that great nation is a wise and discerning people".*[19]
>
> THE MEIRI

Without philosophical foundations, we can be left with unconscious acts of blind – and foreign – worship.

> *Philosophy will lead man from the knowledge of things which are caused and from there he will be able to proceed to knowledge of the Creator.*[20]
>
> HAKHAM ELIA DEL MEDIGO

> *Those who neglect philosophy are lazy and have contempt for the word of God and His Law.*[21]
>
> RABBENU BAHYA

> *The man who has no hint of philosophy goes through life imprisoned in the prejudices derived from common sense, from*

> *the habitual beliefs of his age or his nation, and from convictions which have grown up in his mind without the cooperation or consent of his deliberate reason.*[22]
>
> BERTRAND RUSSELL

Equally true, however, is that without law and ritual we are left with a never-ending sequence of abstract ideas, opinions, and half-truths that bear little practical impact on day-to-day reality.

> *The substantiation of a belief, of a vision of reality, lies in its practical consequence.*[23]
>
> RABBI MATIS WEINBERG

> *The commandments and statutes will lead man to the ultimate good ... the truth of a religion should not be judged by opinions alone.*[24]
>
> HAKHAM ELIA DEL MEDIGO

> *Knowledge, if it does not determine action, is dead to us.*[25]
>
> PLOTINUS

Jewish history bears witness to the disastrous outcomes of those who have failed to balance – or have chosen to disregard – the existential dynamic between philosophy and law, between context and content, between thought and action.

> *I will fight against philosophical opinions that seemingly contradict the Torah, although I think that when the Torah and philosophy are understood correctly, there will be no conflict between them.*[26]
>
> HAKHAM ELIA DEL MEDIGO

References

1. Kli Yakar, Commentary on Bereshit 12:1:3
2. Tzvi Langermann, *Yemenite Midrash*, p. 268
3. Rambam, *Mishneh Torah*, Hilkhot Avodat Kokhavim, 1:1
4. Sanhedrin 102b [William Davidson Talmud, Sefaria.org]
5. Joseph Dweck, *Touring the Talmud*, Aboda Zara. Available online at https://www.sephardi.org.uk/touring-talmud-aboda-zara-41-46-shabbat-ki-tisa/
6. Shimshon Raphael Hirsch, Commentary on Lech Lecha
7. Rambam, *Mishneh Torah*, Hilkhot Avodat Kokhavim 1:3
8. Ya'akov Anatoli, *Malmad haTalmidim*, Miketz, p. 36b
9. Akiva Tatz, *As Dawn Ends the Night*, p. 66
10. Bereshit Rabbah 38. Avraham physically smashed and broke the idols inside his father's shop with a hammer.
11. Yitzhak Ben Moshe Arama, *Akedat Yitzhak*, 45:1:7
12. For a deeper analysis on the new-old nature of Avraham's realisation, read Micah Goodman, *Maimonides & The Book That Changed Judaism*, p. 121
13. Rambam, *Letter to Hasdei haLevi*
14. Shemuel Bornstzain, *Shem Mishmuel*, Shemini
15. According to Rambam, the tribe of Levi continued the practice of circumcision in Egypt, allowing them to physically manifest their commitment to the monotheistic discoveries of their forefather, Avraham (*Mishneh Torah*, Hilkhot Issurei Biah, 13:2).
16. Rambam, *Mishneh Torah*, Hilkhot Avodat Kokhavim, 1:3
17. Avraham Pereira Mendes, *Sermons*, Sermon IX, p. 120
18. Rambam, *Moreh haNevukhim*, 2:31
19. Menahem Meiri, *Magen Avot*, p. 30. This is referenced in Gregg Stern, *Philosophy and Rabbinic Culture*, p. 32
20. Elia Del Medigo, *Behinat ha-Dat*, 77
21. Bahya Ibn Paquda, *Hovot haLevavot*, translated by Menahem Mansour, Introduction, p. 94
22. Bertrand Russell, *The Problems of Philosophy*, Chapter 15
23. Matis Weinberg, *Frameworks: Genesis*, p. 108
24. Elia Del Medigo, *Behinat haDat*, 83-84 (as summarised by Harvey James in *Elia Del Medigo: An Archetype of the Halachic Man?* Tradition, Vol 56, p. 244)
25. Plotinus, *Delphi Complete Works of Plotinus - Complete Enneads*, p. 31
26. Elia Del Medigo, *Behinat haDat*, 19

vayera

וירא

Vayera – *A Testing Lesson*

Vayera introduces us to one of the most perplexing events described in the Torah. Throughout the generations, experts and laymen alike have attempted and struggled to mitigate the ethical, moral, and existential challenges that are entrenched in the story of Avraham and his son, Yitzhak.

Just before we arrive at this *perashah*, we are made aware of the covenant *(berit)* that has been sealed between God and Avraham. It includes a promise that Avraham's descendants will be bountiful and abundant.

> *I will establish My covenant between Me and you, and I will multiply you very greatly. (17:2)*

This promise was a promise based primarily on love.

> *God sees the face of his beloved Avraham in each and every one of his children as a man sees the face of his beloved in the children of his union with his beloved.*[1]
> MICHAEL WYSCHOGROD

> *The election of the Jewish people is the result of God's falling in love with Avraham and founding a family with him.*[2]
> RABBI MEIR SOLOVEICHIK

After desperately waiting for the birth of a child with Sara, Avraham is soon commanded by God to take his beloved child, Yitzhak, and to bind him as an offering.

> *And God said, "Take your son, your only one, whom you love, Yitzhak, and go forth to the land of Moriah, and offer him up as a burnt offering on one of the mountains which I shall say to you." (22:2)*

With this divine request, the promise of Avraham's vast and plentiful offspring seems to be terminated before it even had the opportunity to begin!

> *God had told Avraham that he will be known in history*
> *through Yitzhak. How could such a promise be fulfilled if*
> *Yitzhak were to die now?*[3]
> RADAK

From the outset, it seems as though child sacrifice is on the agenda. Indeed, child sacrifice was nothing new to humanity. The practice of killing children in order to appease a deity dates back to the Meso-American era (10,000-3,500 BCE), and it has found itself a ritualistic role in many cultures.

> *The practice permeated ancient Near Eastern religiosity*
> *throughout the Fertile Crescent, influencing cultures across*
> *north Africa and southern Europe. It is demonstrable in the*
> *archaeological record from as early as the prehistoric periods*
> *and is evident in the textual traditions from the early historical*
> *eras through the first millennium BCE and beyond.*[4]
> ENCYLOPEADIA OF ANCIENT HISTORY

Child sacrifice represents a sick ideology that blinds humanity of sensibility, and views children as the mere property of their parents. Contrary to popular misconception, child sacrifice (as well as any other Torah prohibition) is not merely a *moral* issue, it is primarily an *existential* one. It goes directly against the development of humanity, and this was not to be accepted amongst Yisrael.

> *Child sacrifice and infanticide were common in the heathen*
> *world, but fiercely opposed by the prophets of Yisrael.*[5]
> HAKHAM YOSEF FAUR

> *Idolatrous practice is abhorrent to God, especially the cult of*
> *child-sacrifice.*[6]
> BAHYA BEN ASHER

Indeed, the Torah itself repeatedly polemicises against such cruel and abhorrent behaviour.

> *Anyone among the Israelites, or among the foreigners residing in Israel, who gives any of his offspring to Molekh, shall be doomed to die. (20:2)*
>
> VAYIKRA

> *There shall not be found among you one who passes his son or daughter through fire. (18:10)*
>
> DEVARIM

> *For the people of Yehuda have done what displeases Me – declares God. They have built the shrines of Tophet in the Valley of Ben-hinnom to burn their sons and daughters in fire – which I never commanded, and never entered My mind. (7:30-33)*
>
> YIRMIYAHU

How could the Source of all life – *God* – proscribe such a lifeless outcome?

How could the paragon of kindness – *Avraham* – entertain such an unkind command?

The confusion, it seems, was not lost on Avraham either:

> *Avraham became surprised and said, "These words are confusing. Yesterday you said 'It is through Yitzhak that offspring shall be called for you.'*
> *Then, you went back and said, 'Take your son …'*
> *And now [your angel] says to me, 'Do not lay your hand upon the lad'.*
> *I am bewildered!'*
> *The Holy One, blessed be He responded: "Avraham, I will not violate my covenant or change what I have uttered.*
> *When I said to you 'take your son' I never said to slaughter him. I merely said to 'raise him up.'*

65

> *I said this to you to demonstrate your love, and you did my*
> *bidding. Now take him down.*[7]
>
> BERESHIT RABBAH

Of course, God was not requesting Avraham to *actually* sacrifice his child.[8] Instead, the traumatic episode was to be a simultaneous test and lesson for Avraham and the future generations. The Talmud reaffirms this, stating that God would have never even entertained the prospect of permitting child sacrifice.

> *"And it never entered My mind." (Yirmiyahu 7:33)*
> *– This refers to [the sacrifice of] Yitzhak, the son of*
> *Avraham.*[9]
>
> TALMUD BAVLI

Yitzhak's sacrifice was never a possibility. Rather, God takes Avraham – and us – through this distressing process as an opportunity to teach us about the horror of this terror-laden inheritance from idolatrous generations.

And as willing as Avraham may have seemed to be throughout the episode, there is little doubt that the fatherly emotions within him were bound to overcome his very will to live if such a sacrifice was ever performed.

> *Yitzhak's face was covered in hot tears,*
> *"Dear father, what are you going to say to my mother, when*
> *she does not see me returning with you?"*
> *"Dear son, I know well what will happen to us both …*
> *I and your dear mother, Sara, after your death, will not long*
> *remain on earth,*
> *For who could comfort me in my misery and your mother in*
> *her grief and pain?"*[10]
>
> YUDISHER SHTAM

By reading this rollercoaster of a story involving an established idolatrous ritual of its time, we are taken through a quasi-experiential form of learning.

In other words, the suspense of the very story we read every year is an educational tool that serves as a reminder of the Torah's oft-forgotten but forever relevant objective – weaning Yisrael away from our primal proclivity for idolatry. As they say, old habits die hard.

> *The principal purpose of the Torah is the removal and utter destruction of idolatry.*[11]
>
> RAMBAM

> *Torah's first goal is to eradicate idolatry, both its beliefs and the ritual practices that reinforce those beliefs.*[12]
>
> HOWARD KREISEL

References

1. Michael Wyschogrod, *The Body of Faith*, p. 64
2. Meir Soloveichik, *God's First Love: The Theology of Michael Wyschogrod*. Available online at: https://www.firstthings.com/article/2009/11/gods-first-love-the-theology-of-michael-wyschogrod
3. Radak, Commentary on Bereshit 22:1
4. Jason Tatlock, *Human Sacrifice, Ancient Near East*, Encyclopaedia of Ancient History
5. Jose Faur, *Oedipal Paul*, Mentalities Journal
6. Bahya ben Asher, Commentary on Devarim 12:29
7. Bereshit Rabbah 56:8
8. Rashi follows this interpretation in his Commentary on Bereshit 22:12
9. Ta'anit 4a
10. Jerrold Frakes, *Early Yiddish Texts 1100-1750: With Introduction and Commentary*, p. 316-328; translation from Jerrold Frakes, *Early Yiddish Epic*, p. 149-155
11. Rambam, *Moreh haNevukhim*, 3:29
12. Howard Kreisel, *Judaism As Philosophy*, p. 365

hayye sara

חיי שרה

Hayye Sara – *An Acquisition In Love*

Bereavement has played a significant role throughout human history. The visceral reaction to loss can be both mentally and physically taxing, as the raw nature of bereavement can overwhelm each and every one of us.

These innate reactions arise out of a deep-seated primal mechanism that has evolved to ensure our survival. The strong feelings serve as a reminder about the importance of togetherness.

> *The biological reaction to separation keeps us together because*
> *staying together provides an evolutionary benefit.*[1]
> THE SCIENTIFIC AMERICAN

The modern English word 'bereavement' is derived from two Old English terms:

> *reave, bereafian – to be deprived of something valuable.*
> CHAMBERS DICTIONARY

For Avraham, this definition is all too real. The loss of his beloved Sara epitomised the loss of something he truly valued.

> *Avraham lost the wife who was the darling of his heart.*[2]
> PHILO

> *Sara was united with Avraham in thought, word, and deed.*[3]
> RABBI ADIN STEINSALTZ

Upon Sara's passing, Avraham immediately honours her with a negotiated purchase of a burial field. The term used by the Torah to define this purchase is worth noting, and exploring.

> *The field and the cave that was in it and every tree in the field,*
> *within its boundaries and all around, were passed over to*
> *Avraham as his* ACQUISITION. *(23:17-18)*

This was an acquisition (*miknah*) driven by a deep love for Sara, yet it was an act that simultaneously secured the future of Yisrael's presence on the land, ultimately fulfilling Avraham's covenant with God.

> *The first acquisition of Eretz Yisrael was an act of love, which*
> *set the stamp of Avraham and Sara on the Land for its future.*[4]
> RABBI MATIS WEINBERG

> *It was a transaction of a permanent, enduring nature.*[5]
> RADAK

> *It is as though Jewish marriages were taking place at Sara's*
> *burial place in order to be inspired by the spirit that was alive*
> *in the house of Avraham and Sara, and finding its permanent*
> *expression in this purchase of the burial-lot.*[6]
> RABBI SHIMSHON RAPHAEL HIRSCH

> *This land was to become Avraham's permanent home, here he*
> *and Sara were to have their last resting places. Just as a man's*
> *body was not divided up to be buried in several places, so man*
> *and wife who had shared a happy marriage were never to be*
> *parted in death either.*[7]
> HAKHAM YITZHAK ARAMA

But what does it mean to *acquire*? Has the Torah dealt with an *acquisition* before this episode? What can we learn from the use of this term elsewhere?

The first time we see an acquisition (*miknah*) referred to in the Torah is by Hava, after having given birth to Cain.

> *Now Adam knew his wife Hava, and she conceived and bore*
> *Cain, saying, "I have* ACQUIRED *a male child with the help of*
> *God." (4:1)*

In this context of a child, the term is not merely the static attainment of an entity. Acquiring a child requires constant development, care, and responsibility.

> *When you hold your baby in your arms for the first time, and*
> *you think of all the things you can say and do to influence him,*
> *it's a tremendous responsibility. What you do with him can*
> *influence not only him but everyone he meets, and not for a day*
> *or a month or a year, but for time and eternity.*[8]
>
> ROSE KENNEDY

The second time that the Hebrew root 'to acquire' is referred to in the Torah is by the non-Jewish priest, Malkitzedek of Shalem.

> *He blessed God by saying "Blessed be Avram of God most*
> *high,* ACQUIRER *of heaven and earth." (14:19)*

The term is being used here again in a creative context, now in relation to God – the original Creator – at the helm of heaven and earth. Indeed, every single one of God's acquisitions *(kinyanim)* are things that imply development and care, and not simply the stagnant possessions of an irresponsible and careless owner!

> *Five* ACQUISITIONS *did the Holy One, God,* ACQUIRE *in*
> *His world:*
> *Torah* — *one* ACQUISITION;
> *Heaven and earth* — *one* ACQUISITION;
> *Avraham* — *one* ACQUISITION;
> *Yisrael* — *one* ACQUISITION;
> *The Temple* — *one* ACQUISITION.[9]
>
> PIRKEI AVOT

To truly appreciate what Avraham's acquisition of the land signifies, we can look to these two preceding examples of 'acquisition' in the Torah. In both of these examples, Hava and Malkitzedek use 'acquisition' to denote more than mere ownership, but also development, responsibility, and accountability.

Responsibility equals accountability equals ownership.[10]

PATRICIA SUMMITT

This is a stark reminder of the responsibilities that we, the descendants of Avraham, have in possessing this acquired Land of Yisrael. Even after being away from home for so long, human ingenuity aided in turning a land of desolation into a land of inspiration.

> *A desolation is here that not even imagination can grace with the pomp of life and action. There was hardly a tree or a shrub anywhere. Even the olive and the cactus, those fast friends of the worthless soil, had almost deserted the country.*[11]
>
> MARK TWAIN

However, this physical inheritance is never to be assumed nor neglected. It is to be nourished and developed – especially by our presence on it.

> *Someone told me, 'God willing, we will move to the land of Israel.'*
> *I replied, 'God is certainly willing. What counts is that you be willing.'*[12]
>
> RABBI AVRAHAM YITZHAK KOOK

> *Happy shall you be if you use this time for the good of the Land of Israel, the pride of our past and the luminescence of our future, to fulfil your duty toward it and to help it with all the means and the ways leading to rebuilding its ruins and making its settlement bloom. Remember our pledge to Zion on the rivers of Babylon and our aspiration and prayers to it over all generations. Do not be among those who falter behind its camps; be in the first ranks of its defenders and the fighters for its freedom, and take an important place among its loyal sons and builders.*[13]
>
> HAKHAM MATLOUB ABADI

The fulfilment of our promised return to the land has been very recent, yet our claim to it has its origins in *Hayye Sara*. With this recent development, we must strive to grow out of a petty nationalism based solely on possessing a unique address on the globe. Instead, we must understand that the land finds it source deeply rooted in *love* – the main component of Covenant (*berit*).

> *Every Jew must cherish the Land of Israel and flock to her with a great yearning from the far corners of the earth, as a child rushes to his mother's embrace.*[14]
>
> SEFER HAREDIM

This love must drive us to action. After all, it is the fulfilment of the commandments (*mitzvot*) that renders *Eretz Yisrael* the space of sacredness, the place of purpose.

> *Israel has no intrinsic holiness. It is the commandments, when observed, that confer sanctity upon the land.*[15]
>
> YESHAYAHU LEIBOWITZ

Through Avraham's act of love, we are reminded of the love that must drive our own commitments to the Covenant today and in the future – especially if those commitments are carried out on the land that we have *acquired*.

> *The basis of keeping all the commandments, from the aspect of their inner and ultimate being, can take place only in the land of Israel.*[16]
>
> RABBI AVRAHAM YITZHAK KOOK

Ideas

References

1. Hannah Waters, *The Evolution of Grief,* The Scientific American
2. Philo, *On Abraham,* Book VI, p. 121.
3. Adin Steinsaltz, *Biblical Images: Men and Women of the Book,* p. 21
4. Matis Weinberg, *Frameworks: Genesis,* p. 103
5. Radak, Commentary on Bereshit 23:17
6. Shimshon Raphael Hirsch, Commentary on Hayye Sara
7. Yitzhak ben Moshe Arama, *Akedat Yitzhak,* 22:1
8. Rose Kennedy. As quoted in Hal Donaldson and Kirk Noonan, *Your Next 24 Hours,* Chapter 10
9. Pirkei Avot 6:10
10. Patricia Summitt, *Reach for the Summit,* p. 37
11. Mark Twain, *The Innocents Abroad*
12. Avraham Yitzhak Kook, *Shivkhei haRayah,* p. 208
13. Matloub Abadi, *Magen Ba'adi,* New York 1970, p. 304
14. Elazar Askari, *Sefer Haredim.* As quoted in Mati Alon, *Holocaust & Redemption,* p. 86
15. Yeshayahu Leibowitz, *Judaism, Human Values, and the Jewish State,* p. 121
16. Avraham Yitzhak Kook, *Eretz Hefetz,* p. 31

toledot

תולדות

Toledot – *Beyond Matter*

The thought of twins usually conjures up images of resemblance and sameness. The story of Ya'akov and Esav, the twin sons of Rivka and Yitzhak, does the opposite.

The non-identical nature of these twins expresses many of the opposing forces that we grapple with as humans: nature versus nurture, ownership versus responsibility, transaction versus relationship, meaning versus nihilism, the moment versus the future.

The events of the *perashah* are all rooted in Rivka, the quintessential mother of Yisrael, as she plots behind the scenes to influence the outcome of events. First, we are introduced to the birth of her twin boys, Esav and Ya'akov.

> *And when her time was come to give birth, there were twins in [Rivka's] womb.*
> *The first one came out ruddy; like a hairy mantle all over, and they called his name 'Esav'.*
> *Then his brother came out, his hand grasping Esav's heel, and they called his name 'Ya'akov'. (25:25-26)*

The description in the Torah makes sure to highlight the fact that the twins are fraternal – not identical. This explains the consistently stark contrasts between them as they develop into adulthood.

> *Esav was a cunning hunter, a man of the field, and Ya'akov was a simple man, a dweller in tents. (25:27)*

As a hungry Esav returns home from his usual day of hunting, murdering, and raping, he demands his simple brother Ya'akov to feed him the food that he was preparing. Before Ya'akov consents, he wants Esav to sell him his inheritance (*bekhora*) in return.

> *Ya'akov prepared a stew and Esav came from the field, and he*
> *was famished.*
> *And Esav said to Ya'akov, "Let me gulp down some of this red*
> *red stuff, for I am famished."... Ya'akov said, "Sell now your*
> *birthright to me."*
> *And Esav said, "Look, I am going to die, so why do I need a*
> *birthright?" (25:29-32)*

The wild-natured Esav is quick to accept this asymmetric exchange with zero hesitation. Esav's urge-over-thought reaction is symptomatic of the chaotic consciousness *(tohu)* that the *kabbalists* believed he possessed.[1]

But what did this type of birthright or inheritance really entail? Why was Ya'akov so eager to obtain it, and why was Esav so content with giving it away?

First, let us consider the kinship-based society of the Ancient Near East, which found twins to be disruptive to the normal order of lineage. As Esav was the first twin to emerge from the womb, he was the brother who was entitled to a double portion of his father Yitzhak's inheritance. Indeed, this was the law as practiced throughout the ancient world prior to Torah law.

> *When brothers are dividing their father's estate, the firstborn*
> *son shall choose and take two portions as his portion, and*
> *thereafter his brothers, in turn, choose and take theirs.*[2]
> ASSYRIAN LAW

> *The extra portion given to the first-born was one of the ethical*
> *concerns which were practiced as a matter of custom before the*
> *giving of the Torah.*[3]
> HAKHAM NATANEL BEN YESHAYA

Ever since then, inheritance has referred to the transfer of physical matter – money, land, jewellery – determined by biological descent. However, the inheritance *(bekhora)* referred to in *Toledot* goes beyond physics, and beyond biology. The *contents* may consist of material benefits such as land, but the *context* of it is a familial plot filled with meaningful obligations and existential purpose. *Bekhora* reflects an integrated system that allows a holistic identity to be transmitted across the generations.

> *The brothers were not concerned about their financial inheritance nor did Ya'akov pursue the firstborn for a position of honour. The entire effort here was to determine who would inherit the blessing of Avraham: that God would be with him and his descendants to give them the inheritance of the Land. This was the 'wealth and riches' that Yitzhak inherited from Avraham. Not the material wealth of herds and other benefits.*[4]
>
> ABARBANEL

> *Know, first, who you are, and then adorn yourself accordingly.*[5]
>
> EPICTETUS

> *All material wealth available to man can endure only if its very possession rests on durable foundations.*[6]
>
> HAKHAM YITZHAK ARAMA

Esav understood this responsibility, and he was clearly not willing to take it upon himself. The momentary satisfaction of physical satiation (in this case, food) was more important to him. His ideology rings the same tune as what the nihilists of today benignly exclaim: *"since we are all doomed to perish, should we not enjoy the instant pleasures of a world that ultimately bears little significance?"*

> *And Esav said, "Look, I am going to die, so why do I need a birthright?"*
> (25:32)

Esav, by sacrificing the future for the present, is embodying the exact *reverse* of the earlier sacrifice that his grandfather Avraham was willing to take with Yitzhak at the altar.

> *You don't do reverse sacrifices. That's a very bad idea. It eradicates the possibility that you will bring the most noble being into existence.*[7]
>
> DR JORDAN PETERSON

Indeed, Ya'akov understood that Esav's animalistic urge for instantaneous pleasure does not mesh with the responsible legacy of Avraham.

> *The mass of mankind is evidently quite slavish in their tastes, preferring a life suitable to beasts… and instant pleasures.*[8]
>
> ARISTOTLE

> *It is in responsibility that most people find the meaning that sustains them through life. It is not in impulsive pleasure.*[9]
>
> DR JORDAN PETERSON

> *Esav lacks the discipline of self-sacrifice for a significant future benefit that those rights may provide for his children. He is focused on his present personal gratification, unconcerned for family loyalty, lacking respect for tradition and inconsiderate of the welfare of his progeny.*[10]
>
> RABBI MOSHE SHAMAH

Once Ya'akov understood this, the opportunity for him to be the next link in the developing chain of Yisrael trumped everything – even if it meant nefariously taking his brother's blessing from his father Yitzhak, by pretending to be Esav!

> *Ya'akov came close to Yitzhak his father and he felt him and he said, "The voice is the voice of Ya'akov, and the hands are the hands of Esav."*
> *Yitzhak did not recognize him, because his hands were hairy like those of his brother Esav, and he blessed him. And he said, "Are you my son Esav?" And Yitzhak said, "I am." (27:22-24)*

Throughout the generations, the strategy that Ya'akov executed in order to receive his brother's blessing has been debated with passion, and sometimes equated with deceit.

Ya'akov's conduct seems hard to understand. He who was to become the fountainhead of the Jewish nation appears guilty of the vilest accusation.[11]

HAKHAM YITZHAK ARAMA

Let us cling to the belief that the motives of Ya'akov were laudable – that he really feared to see the patriarchal power descend into his brother's unhallowed hands.[12]

HAKHAM AVRAHAM PEREIRA MENDES

However, we must be honest enough to accept that life presents us with choices that are not always ideal. *Toledot* teaches us that the correct decision ultimately rests on a realistic analysis of the consequences of each choice.

Who is the wise man? Rabbi Shimon says it is he who foresees the consequence.[13]

PIRKEI AVOT

The proper moral decision is not always between good and evil; sometimes it is between a greater and a lesser evil.[14]

RABBI ELHANAN SAMET

Toledot also reminds us that physics and biology – alone – do not determine the grand responsibility of continuity. This whole episode highlights the meaning behind committing to a long-term vision of life based on legacy and responsibility, while reminding us of the meaninglessness inherent in a life lacking purpose and identity. This is food for thought in a world where the erosion of fundamental aspects of human identity is taking place before our very eyes.

The least of things with a meaning are worth more in life than the greatest of things without it.[15]

CARL JUNG

Afterall, the inheritance of an identity is more than just leaving something *for* people – it is leaving something *in* people.

What we know matters, but who we are matters more.[16]

BRENÉ BROWN

Ideas

References

1. Etz Hayyim, *Hechal haNikudim*, Sha'ar 8
2. Assyrian Law, Tablet 1. This appears in Ziva Maximov's *Law and Society in the Bible*, Chapter 2.2
3. Natanel Ben Yeshaya, *Nur al-Zalam*. Available in Tzvi Langermann, *Yemenite Midrash*, p. 123
4. Abarbanel, Commentary on Toledot
5. Epictetus, *Enchiridion*, Volume 2, Chapter 1, p. 7
6. Yitzhak Ben Moshe Arama, *Akedat Yitzhak*, 24:1
7. Jordan Peterson, *Biblical Series XIII*, Jacob's Ladder (Transcript)
8. Aristotle, *Nicomachean Ethics*, 1095b 20
9. Jordan Peterson, *Finding Meaning in Responsibility*. Available online: https://www.youtube.com/watch?v=BIVec7zOCEU
10. Moshe Shamah, *Recalling the Covenant*, Toledot, p. 126
11. Yitzhak Ben Moshe Arama, *Akedat Yitzhak*, 23:1
12. Avraham Pereira Mendes, *Sermons*, Sermon IV, p. 47
13. Pirkei Avot, 2:9
14. Elhanan Samet, *Moral Dimension*. Available online: https://www.etzion.org.il/en/moral-dimension-story-yitzchaks-blessings
15. Carl Jung, *Modern Man in Search of a Soul*, p. 67
16. Brené Brown, *Daring Greatly*, Introduction

vayetze

ויצא

Vayetze – Grounded Transcendency

Homo sapien has craved transcendency since time immemorial. The transcendent experience is an interaction with something greater than one's self, and it has played a role in almost every culture throughout history.

> It has often seemed as if the longing we have for spiritual enlightenment is in direct proportion to its distance, its foreignness, its unfamiliarity. We prefer the far to the near.[1]
> RABBI JONATHAN SACKS

> Man is partly empirical, partly transcendental.[2]
> CARL JUNG

Many have achieved such enlightened states through a variety of sometimes questionable means: meditation, music, or psychedelics. Though it was once considered a pathological state, the latest neuroscientific research highlights the naturality of it all.

Transcendent experiences can provide temporary moments of truth, clarity, and guidance. They are akin to the sudden appearance of a bright light in a dark room that helps one temporarily map out the contents of that room with clarity...just before darkness takes over again once the light departs.

> At times the truth shines so brilliantly that we perceive it as clear as day. Our nature and habit then draw a veil over our perception, and we return to a darkness almost as dense as before. We are like those who, though beholding frequent flashes of lightning, still find themselves in the thickest darkness of the night.[3]
> RAMBAM

In *Vayetze*, Ya'akov achieves transcendental enlightenment after he leaves home to embark on a new stage of his life. He falls asleep, and has a dream that will end up shaping the course of history.

> *Ya'akov came upon a certain place and stopped there for the*
> *night, for the sun had set, and he took one of the stones of the*
> *place and put it at his head and he lay down in that place, and*
> *he dreamed.*
> *Look, a ladder was set against the ground with its top reaching*
> *the heavens, and, look, messengers of God were going up and*
> *coming down it. And, look, the Lord was poised over him…*
> *(28:11-13)*

Ladders with messengers...nested levels of reality...the presence of God – these are all hallmarks of a transcendent experience.

> *Ya'akov slumbers, and while his wearied frame reposes in*
> *sleep, there breaks upon him a vision of heavenly import, with*
> *all the indications of a supernal, awe-inspiring visitation.*[4]
> HAKHAM AVRAHAM PEREIRA MENDES

But are we really meant to take such a dream seriously? Afterall, dreams are merely the result of electrical impulses that involve neurotransmitters acting upon neural receptors. When reduced down to its individual components, the transcendency achieved through a dream is inseparable from material reality.

So, since we can reduce and explain the underlying mechanism of a dream, is it not the case that such an emergent phenomenon is meaningless or unreal?

Absolutely not. We dare do that with love, and we dare do that with dreams.

> *Romantic love can be traced to such physiological processes as*
> *the firing of dopamine and oxytocin, yet love is made no less*
> *real or meaningful thereby.*[5]
> GREGORY GORELIK

Rightfully so, what follows for Ya'akov after this moment of transcendence is a mixture of wonder, awe and – most significantly – existential realisation.

*And Ya'akov awoke from his sleep and he said, "Indeed, the
Lord is in this place, and I did not know."
And he was afraid, and he said, "How fearsome is this place!
This is none other than the house of God, and this is the gate
of the heavens." (28:16-17)*

Ya'akov's frightening realisation is what Torah refers to as 'the fear of God'
– the ego-dissolving moment an individual can experience upon
encountering the divine reality that exists beyond human limits.

*Transcendent experiences bring perspective, helping us
to abandon the conceit that we are at the centre of the world.*[6]
EMILY ESFAHANI SMITH

It is this same sense of fear, or existential awareness, that can trigger an
individual's receptivity to begin acknowledging something greater than
themselves.

The fear of the Lord is the beginning of wisdom.[7]
TEHILLIM

Indeed, 'the fear of God' is a far more sophisticated concept than how it is
commonly presented today in "pop" Torah: juvenile promises of dread and
terror, correlated with the level of knowledge that one has about God and
His world.

*In accordance with one's knowledge will be the love of God –
if much knowledge, then much love, and if little knowledge,
then little love.*[8]
RAMBAM

But what is Ya'akov meant to do after such an awesome realisation? How
does he respond having just experienced transcendency?

*And Ya'akov rose early in the morning and took the stone that
he had put at his head, and he set it as a pillar and poured oil
over its top…*

> "This stone, which I have set up as a pillar, shall be a house of
> God, and everything that You give me I will surely tithe it to
> you." *(28:18 & 22)*

Ya'akov, by consecrating upon which he dreamt with oil, immediately converts the *otherworldly* experience into a financial act that has *earthly* benefits.

> *Ya'akov translates the experience into tithes (ma'aser)
> promising that he will tithe all his physical possessions. He 'de-
> religionizes' his experience, understanding that being religious
> cannot mean withdrawing from this world. It must
> mean engaging with this world.*[9]
>
> RABBI NATHAN LOPEZ CARDOZO

Throughout our own lives, we may experience ephemeral moments of transcendency where the raw realisation of something greater than ourselves will capture us, just like it did for Ya'akov. This can happen to us while praying, partaking in ritual, or gazing at the selfless beauty of Creation.

After all, our physical world has limits that only emergent and ephemeral phenomena such as awe and imagination can sense. These experiences belong to a supra-rational realm that exists beyond our understanding. Indeed, many practical *kabbalistic* schools of thought believe that they can tap into and affect the mechanisms of this 'upper realm', through practices and actions derived from the chief text of *kabbalah*, the *Zohar*.

> *Practical kabbalah concerns the actual manipulation of
> spiritual forces through the intervention of a mystic.*[10]
>
> NAFTALI LOEWENTHAL

However, the existence of supra-rational experiences do not warrant an invitation to manipulate other worlds, or to reside in them. We must be grounded in the reality on earth *(olam hazeh)*. It is no wonder that God stresses the earthliness of even the Torah itself.

> *[The Torah] is not in the heavens. (30:12)*
>
> DEVARIM

Fixating on the supposed happenings of the upper realms can develop to a point where the physical realm is not worth properly interacting with, or investing in. This can impact our practice, our beliefs, and our lives – even in the garb of piety.

> *Most people have a distorted understanding of what piety consists of, assuming it to be limited to recitation of many psalms, long confessions, indulging in severe fasts, and undergoing immersions in snow and ice, all of which are incompatible with sound reason.*[11]
>
> RAMHAL

> *The Torah has taught us proper behaviour, namely, that a person should not depart too much from earthly custom and nature. Even a prophet returns to his original situation once he has left the prophetic state.*[12]
>
> HAKHAM DAVID ADANI

It is precisely this risk that led some of our greatest Jewish communities, and some of our greatest legal codifiers, to avoid the mixing of earthliness with otherworldliness.

> *Western Sepharadim distanced themselves from kabbalistic studies, stressing instead the need for rational philosophy.*[13]
>
> HAKHAM MARC ANGEL

> *Rabbi Yosef Karo's mystical life did not spill over into his daylight activities. The Karo of the codes and the responsa remained healthy, realistic, and down to earth.*[14]
>
> ZWI WERBLOWSKY

> *I have not merited understanding ... that the words of all the well-known legal authorities should be discarded, and the words of the [kabbalist] Arizal should be held as though it is law given to Moshe at Sinai ... from where do you learn this?*[15]
>
> HAKHAM OVADIA YOSEF

What Ya'akov does in *Vayetze* is use a *non-physical* experience of transcendence as a way of affecting the *physical* world. He does not choose to abandon the physical world for 'a life in the sky', nor does he expect to manipulate non-physical realms through his actions. This care and concern can make all the difference.

> When I read the Zohar and decide that because this is what it says in the Zohar that I am going to do X as a result of it, and I bring it straight down to practical action, without thinking about the fact that these abstractions need to develop appropriately, and that I'm going to lose a huge amount by bringing it down into the concrete, is when we get the problems. And these problems, are problems.[16]
>
> RABBI JOSEPH DWECK

Ya'akov reminds us that no matter how ephemeral our experiences may be, the Torah ultimately requires of us to remain grounded on earth – because it is there that life takes place.

References

1. Jonathan Sacks, *Covenant & Conversation*, Nitzavim 5776
2. Carl Jung, *Mysterium Coniunctionis*, p. 765
3. Rambam, *Moreh haNevukhim*, Introduction
4. Avraham Pereira Mendes, *Sermons*, Sermon IV
5. Gregory Gorelik, *The Evolution and Exploitation of Transcendence*, Introduction
6. Emily Esfahani Smith, *The Power of Meaning*. Available online at: https://www.thecut.com/article/what-a-transcendent-experience-really-means.html
7. Tehillim, 112:10
8. Rambam, *Mishneh Torah*, Hilkhot Teshuva 10:6
9. Nathan Lopez Cardozo, *Jewish Law as Rebellion*, Vayetze
10. Naftali Loewenthal, *Communicating the Infinite*, p. 7
11. Ramhal, *Mesilat Yesharim*, Introduction
12. David Adani, *Midrash haGadol*. Available in Tzvi Langermann, *Yemenite Midrash*, p. 129
13. Marc Angel, *Sephardic Customs*, p. 7
14. Zwi Werblowsky, *Joseph Caro*, p. 286
15. Ovadia Yosef, *Yabia Omer*, Orah Hayyim 2:25. Here, Hakham Ovadia Yosef is expressing his surprise as to why certain people would hold *kabbalistic* practices above that of the legal practices that were established by Rabbi Yosef Karo's seminal legal code (*Shulkhan Arukh*). Hakham Ovadia Yosef's books were banned and burned by zealots during his lifetime.
16. Joseph Dweck, *Rationalist vs Mystical Judaism*. Available online at: https://www.youtube.com/watch?v=KjGl4Ep2B5U&t

vayishlah

וישלח

Vayishlah – *Unilateral Initiatives*

Up until very recent times, the people of Yisrael have rarely been considered as strong-handed or assertive power-players.

Vayishlah opens up with a scene that seems to epitomise the historical perception of Jewish subservience. Ya'akov – who evolves to become, and be named, *Yisrael* – anxiously prepares for a meeting with his antithetical brother Esav, for the first time in twenty years.

> *"Ya'akov was greatly afraid, and he was distressed..."* (32:8)
> *– Ya'akov prepared for three things: a gift, prayer, and war.*
>
> RASHI

It is worth being reminded why Ya'akov is so nervous about meeting Esav again, considering what Esav had vowed earlier!

> *And Esav seethed with resentment against Ya'akov over the blessing his father had blessed him, and Esav said in his heart, "As soon as the time for mourning for my father comes round, I will kill my brother Ya'akov."* (27:41)

It seems as though the topic of inheritance has been a point of contention for time immemorial!

> *When it comes to inheritance, the politest men quarrel.*[1]
> RALPH WALDO EMERSON
>
> *Men sooner forget the death of their father than the loss of their inheritance.*[2]
> NICCOLO MACHIAVELLI

It is still surprising to see Ya'akov displaying fear and preparing himself, even after receiving assurances from God as to his safety and security. Is there anything to learn from this?

> *The fear of Ya'akov teaches us that God's promises are not to be considered as ironclad guarantees, as valid under all circumstances. Indeed, God's omnipotence allows Him to determine the outcome of all our endeavours, but human intelligence and willpower would be utterly meaningless were they not to play a significant part in determining the success or failure of our endeavours.*[3]
>
> HAKHAM YITZHAK OF ARAMA

Hope in the divine *(bitahon)* must always be tethered to efforts by the human *(hishtadlut)*. That is, ultimately, the assurance of our free will.

And so, it is no wonder that Ya'akov ends up initiating the conversation with Esav, appeasing him with physical gifts and verbal tributes in an attempt to silence the anticipated fury of his brother.

> *Ya'akov took from what came into his hand a gift for his brother Esav:*
> *Two hundred female and twenty male goats, two hundred ewes and twenty rams, thirty milch camels with their young, forty cows and ten bulls, twenty female donkeys and ten male donkeys. (32:14-16)*

Should a potential threat such as Esav really be met with gifts and grovelling? Is Ya'akov exhibiting weakness at a time that demands strength?

The reality, as is often the case, is not what it seems on the surface.

What this episode actually demonstrates is far more sophisticated than a microscopic analysis that suggests mere capitulation. When we zoom out to a macroscopic observation, we can appreciate Ya'akov's high level of emotional intelligence, and his early application of the sociological theory of 'unilateral initiatives'.

Unilateral initiatives – such as gift-giving – are intended to overcome hostility and impasse by eliciting trust and thereby allowing for positive behaviour.[4]

THE JOURNAL OF SOCIAL PSYCHOLOGY

Ya'akov realized that he must use every effort to reach reconciliation.[5]

RABBI MOSHE SHAMAH

Ya'akov prepares for the hostile impasse that exists with Esav, and he understands that trust is critical to overcome it – especially since reciprocity from Esav is far from assured.

By tapping into Esav's primal drive for self-interest and short-term gratitude, Ya'akov offers gifts and tributes in order to induce trust. This trust will ultimately decrease Esav's potentially punitive behaviour, and prevent a physical battle.

The supreme art of war is to subdue the enemy without fighting.[6]

SUN TZU

Indeed, gift-giving has played a significant role in human civilisation, and has been shown to provide evolutionary benefits.

Paleolithic man exchanged primitive tools such as animal teeth and shaped rocks in order to form a web of social connectivity. The ancient Egyptians offered gifts to their deities, as well as to their Pharaohs on coronation days. The ancient Greeks offered gifts to their gods for battlefield protection, and to people who were celebrating birthdays in order to ward off evil spirits that supposedly haunt them.

It is only until the Middle Ages (5th-15th century) where we begin to see gift-giving as a common and successful way of fostering important social interactions and political allegiances. Ya'akov may have been ahead of his time!

Indeed, this strategy was not lost on our people throughout a challenging history living amongst the nations of the world.

> *Ya'akov formulated the fundamental basis of Jewish survival*
> *among unfriendly nations: economic self-interest.*[7]
>
> RABBI MATIS WEINBERG

It is for this reason that Ya'akov's strategy is considered recommended reading – and recommended practice – for those in similar standoffs.

> *It is permissible to flatter the evildoers in this world, and we*
> *learn this from Ya'akov.*[8]
>
> TALMUD BAVLI

> *Whoever wishes to placate a king or a government, but does*
> *not know their policy nor can he predict their attitudes – let*
> *him place this story [of Ya'akov and Esav] before him and*
> *learn from it.*[9]
>
> MIDRASH LEKAH TOV

> *It has never been permitted to honour the wicked, except for*
> *terror, that is to say, if one is afraid that the wicked man will*
> *injure him or cause him a loss at a time when the hand of the*
> *wicked is mighty.*[10]
>
> ORHOT TZADIKIM

Ya'akov is aware that gift-*giving* has implicit strings attached to it, strings which may very well ensure survival in the face of adversity.

It seems, however, that Esav was equally aware of the implicit strings that are attached to gift-*acceptance*, as he initially refuses the gifts and tributes. Given Esav's defensive reaction to receiving the gifts, maybe he was conscious of the implicit burden of debt that falls upon the gift-acceptor?

> *Esav said, "I have much, my brother. Keep what you have."*
> (33:9)

The sense of obligation can be incredibly powerful!

Vayishlah ultimately reminds us of the power behind utilising the rational pursuit of self-interest to prevent and defuse conflicts. This strategy, however, can only work if one has a strong sense of self, security, and emotional intelligence.

Most people could not carry out such a plan. Personal pride and ego would not allow us to act subservient. Only a person who is very secure can succeed in such circumstances. A secure person knows that self-worth is not determined by the perceptions of others. It is a consequence of our real substance. Yaakov had this security. This quality allowed him to develop and carry out a successful strategy.[11]

RABBI BERNARD FOX

However, when faced with a situation that requires defusing, we should always be cognisant of the fine line that exists between being emotionally intelligent, and self-degrading; between virtue, and vice.

The difference is "too nice" - where ends the virtue or begins the vice.[12]

ALEXANDER POPE

References

1. Ralph Waldo Emerson, *The Complete Works of Ralph Waldo Emerson*
2. Niccolo Machiavelli, *The Prince,* Chapter 17
3. Yitzhak Ben Moshe Arama, *Akedat Yitzhak,* 26:1
4. Michael Large, *The Journal of Social Psychology,* Vol. 62, No. 3
5. Moshe Shamah, *Recalling the Covenant,* Vayishlah, p. 154
6. Sun Tzu, *The Art of War,* Chapter 3
7. Matis Weinberg, *Frameworks: Genesis,* Vayishlah
8. Sotah 41b
9. Tobiah Ben Eliezer, *Midrash Lekah Tov*
10. *Orhot Tzadikim,* 24:22
11. Bernard Fox, *Rabbi Fox on Parsha (OU Torah),* Vayishlah. Available online at: https://outorah.org/p/306/
12. Alexander Pope, *The Poetical Works of Alexander Pope,* p. 186

vayeshev

וישב

Vayeshev – Dignity In Difference

Vayeshev (literally, "he settled") is arguably the most unsettling of all Torah portions. Within one story, we are taken through the complete gamut of the human experience.

From Ya'akov's expressions of love for his son Yosef, to the jealousy of the brothers, the shame of their fateful actions, and the shared hatred that binds them together, up until they reach a point of despair, shock, and surprise. Amidst this concoction of emotional states, there are two characters that teach us more about our people's past, present, and future than any other duo in the Torah – Yehuda and Yosef.

Ya'akov – now *Yisrael* – finds himself involved in yet another sibling conflict that has been brewing internally between his twelve sons. Yosef, the eleventh of the twelve sons, is the subject of the tension.

> *Yisrael [Ya'akov] loved Yosef more than all his sons ... And his brothers saw that their father loved Yosef more than all his brothers, and they hated him and could not speak a kind word to him. (37:4-5)*

Jealousy – that self-inflicted sickness – is the catalyst to impending domestic violence. After feeling side-lined by their own father, the brothers are led by Yehuda to plot and take revenge on the favoured Yosef.

> *And so now, let us kill him [Yosef] and fling him into of the pits, and we can say that a vicious beast has devoured him ... (37:20)*

A cursory reading of this story suggests that this is a familial dispute that has arisen as a result of parental favouritism or preferential treatment. Yet at its core, the conflict between Yehuda and Yosef cuts much deeper:

> *This conflict is not something that happened to a small family*
> *in Canaan. The fight between Yosef and Yehuda became what*
> *defines Yisrael. This is us.*[1]
>
> RABBI JOSEPH DWECK

To truly understand the ramifications of this brotherly battle, we must look to the differences that defined Yehuda and Yosef back then, and their ideological descendants today.

Yehuda is a wary protectionist who is short on charisma but long on accountability. His raison d'etre lies not in dreaming new possibilities, but rather in reacting to current circumstances.

> *Yosef's antagonists believed that Yisrael could flourish only in*
> *isolation, forming the world while remaining unformed by it.*
> *But holiness is genuine only when grown from the earth,*
> *expressive of the inner beauty of Creation's potential. Piety*
> *without vitality is like a soul without a body and a colour*
> *without a rose.*[2]
>
> RABBI MATIS WEINBERG

Contrast Yehuda to the *"youthful"* and *"beautiful"* Yosef, a renowned *"dreamer"* known to be colourful in thought as well as in clothing. Beauty was important to Yosef, but not the type of selfish beauty that dominates contemporary society.

> *The only reason that beauty ever breaks down into something*
> *unwholesome is when we end up perverting it for our own*
> *personal use; when we look at something beautiful and think*
> *"we can have that."*[3]
>
> RABBI JOSEPH DWECK

When Yosef is called to lead, it is precisely his combination of vision, creativity, and charisma that gives Egypt the chance of survival at an existentially-defining moment in its history. Indeed, it is exactly these traits of *Yosef the integrator* that *Yehuda the isolationist* firmly believed would lead Yisrael towards nihilism or, in today's parlance, *"off the derekh"*.

Now if one was to guess which brother – Yehuda or Yosef – is the mascot of faithfulness, piety, and holiness, it could surely not be Yosef? After all, Yosef's dynamic traits seem antithetical to the stasis that characterises much of contemporary religiosity.

So why is it that Yosef was Yisrael's *"favourite"*, and why is that our tradition speaks so highly of Yosef?

> *All of Yisrael is called by the name of Yosef, as it says "Perhaps*
> *God will grace the remnant of Yosef."* [4]
>
> MIDRASH TEHILLIM

The reason is subtle, yet profound.

> *Yosef is committed to God, but he never predefines his*
> *approach to God – because you cannot do such a thing.*
> *The way of God, of Existence, is that you constantly have to be*
> *checking out what He is doing.*
> *You must always be in questioning mode: "where is God,*
> *where is Existence, going now?"*
> *The minute you decide "this" is what is going on, and you*
> *decide to live your entire life according to that perception – you*
> *remove yourself from any relationship with God.*
> *The more rigid one becomes in their perception of the world,*
> *the less sensitive they are to the beauty and creativity that Yosef*
> *is sensitive to.* [5]
>
> RABBI JOSEPH DWECK

Throughout the *parashiyot* that relate to him, we notice that Yosef has a unique capacity to look outwards and to approximate the changing nature of the real world. This provides him with the tools to lead, and to offer solutions to challenges posed by the unexpected developments of an ever-changing world.

> *Life is under no obligation to give us what we expect.* [6]
>
> MARGARET MITCHELL

There is still much for us to learn from Yosef today, as we are witnessing the development of sociological, scientific, and political realities that we as a people can either choose to ominously ignore, or carefully address.

Yosef's ability to respond to reality on reality's terms – *not his own* – is a key factor in his decision-making. For Yehuda, however, everything was predefined, predetermined, and unchanging. Yosef's strategy leaves him vulnerable and open, while Yehuda's strategy appears secure and protected.

It is therefore ironic to discover that all the fears that Yehuda had about Yosef's approach were ironically actualised through Yehuda himself! It is the 'dangerous' Yosef who controls his sexual desires after receiving immodest proposals from women[7], while Yehuda gives in and takes women as prostitutes.[8] It is the 'risky' Yosef who warns his brothers of the cultural norms of foreign societies[9], while Yehuda risked *"dangerous mingling with gentiles"*.[10] It is the 'careless' Yosef who marries a woman from within the camp of Yisrael[11], while Yehuda marries a Canaanite.[12] It is Yosef's son (Ephraim) who grows to become a role model[13], while Yehuda's sons (Er and Onan) are killed as a result of their sexual immorality.[14]

> *Vayeshev furnishes a follow-up survey of the pragmatic ramifications of Yehuda and Yosef's respective views within the real world, in a fabulous contrast of personal histories that the youthful, beautiful, and dangerous dreamer [Yosef] wins hands down.*[15]
>
> RABBI MATIS WEINBERG

The fundamental question facing our people today is not about which approach – Yehuda's or Yosef's – is the right one. There is a time and a place for both ... as well as the sixty-eight other approaches.

> *There are seventy approaches to Torah.*[16]
>
> BAMIDBAR RABBAH

Rather, the issue at hand is that we seem to have forgotten the very existence of Yosef's approach – an approach that is much needed at a time wherein a black and white mentality has dulled the colourful creativity and nuance that is required for any entity to remain cutting-edge, responsive, and relevant.

We have regained possession of our promised land, and we are transitioning back from being a religion to being a nation. Our response to the beauty of this reality should not be unidimensional. We can incorporate our recent status in history as *isolationist Jews* (Yehuda), with our new status as *integrator Israelites* (Yosef/Yisrael).

> For the first time in 4000 years, Jews have sovereignty and independence in Israel, freedom and equality in the Diaspora. Shall we act as if we were still in the nineteenth century, not the twenty-first?[17]
>
> RABBI JONATHAN SACKS

As the prophet Yehezkel states so movingly,

> Take a piece of wood and write on it, "For Yehuda…" and take another piece of wood and write on it, "For Yosef…"
> Draw them close, one to the other… and they shall become one in your hand. For I shall make them one nation in your land.[18]
>
> YEHEZKEL

The survival and strength of a nation, a culture, a religion is influenced by its careful and creative integration of eternal principles with new details.

Yehuda – justifiably so – wrote our people's most recent chapter. It is now time for Yosef to dream – and to write our next one.

> Hold fast to dreams,
> For if dreams die
> Life is a broken-winged bird,
> That cannot fly.[19]
>
> LANGSTON HUGHES

Ideas

References

1. Joseph Dweck, *Vayeshev 5763*, Audio Shiur available on 'RJD' mobile application on the App Store.
2. Matis Weinberg, *Frameworks: Genesis*, p. 239. For an analysis on the differences between Yehuda and Yosef, read this essay in full.
3. Joseph Dweck, *Vayeshev 5763*, Audio Shiur available on 'RJD' mobile application on the App Store.
4. Midrash Tehillim 3:3, based on Amos 5:15
5. Joseph Dweck, *Vayeshev 5763*, Audio Shiur available on 'RJD' mobile application on the App Store.
6. Attributed to Margaret Mitchell
7. Bereshit, 39:12
8. Bereshit, 38:15,16
9. Bereshit, 46:34
10. Bereshit, 38:1, and Rashi's commentary
11. Bereshit, 41:45
12. Bereshit, 38:2, and Radak's commentary
13. Bereshit, 41:52
14. Bereshit, 38:7,10
15. Matis Weinberg, *Frameworks: Genesis*, p. 237
16. Bamidbar Rabbah, 13:15-16; Also stated by Rabbi Akiva, *Otiyyot de-Rabbi Akiva*; Avraham Ibn Ezra, *Commentary on the Torah*, Introduction; Nahmanides, Commentary on Bereshit 8:4
17. Jonathan Sacks, *A Judaism Engaged with the World*, p. 14
18. Yehezkel, 37:16-25
19. Langston Hughes, *Dreams*

miketz

מקץ

Miketz – Beyond Wisdom

Miketz presents us with an ironic twist of fate, as Yosef is saved from the pits of Egypt thanks to the same dangerous business that got him there in the first place – dreams. Yosef *the dreamer* becomes Yosef *the dream interpreter*, as he is tasked with interpreting Pharoah's mysterious dreams.

> *And Pharaoh said to Yosef, "I dreamed a dream, and none can solve it, and I have heard about you that you can understand a dream to solve it." (41:15)*

Dream interpretation was a serious and sacred business in ancient Egypt, with the first written record dating back to 1300BC. The ancient Egyptians believed that our eyes are opened in our dreams – to advice, threats, and warnings. Accordingly, the Egyptian word for 'dream' was symbolised with the hieroglyphic image of an open eye.

> *In ancient Egypt, the word 'dream' not only refers to 'see something in a dream', but also means 'to awaken', representing dreaming as a special state of consciousness, something like 'watching during sleep'.[1]*
> THE JOURNAL OF DREAM RESEARCH

Egyptian wizards and sages would be tasked with interpreting dreams, taking directions from their chief text of dream interpretation. These are likely the very same wizards and sages that Pharoah calls upon to help him, but who fail to do so.

> *It happened in the morning that Pharoah's heart pounded, and he sent and called in all the wizards and all the sages of Egypt, and Pharaoh recounted to them his dream, but no one could solve them for Pharoah. (41:8)*

When Pharoah turns to Yosef, who ends up accurately interpreting the dream, he appoints him to manage the impending manifestation of the dream.

> *Pharaoh's dreams are a metaphor for the next 14 years of Egypt's fate. The country is to experience seven years of abundant agricultural production, followed by seven years of famine. Pharoah appoints Yosef to prepare Egypt for the famine during the years of abundance.[2]*
>
> RABBI ARYEH KLAPPER

This outcome begs the following question: why was it that the Egyptian wizards and sages failed to see what a Hebrew slave so clearly described?

> *We have reason to wonder why these great wise men of Egypt were unable to come up with a better interpretation of Pharaoh's dream.[3]*
>
> BAHYA BEN ASHER

The answer may become clearer once we analyse the difference between the wisdom of Egypt, and the beauty of Yosef.

Let us first define what a sage and a wizard really are.

> *Sage – a person who is wise through reflection and experience. Wizard (wise + ard) – a person skilled in magic, archaically known as a wise person.*
>
> MERRIAM-WEBSTER DICTIONARY

A wizard and a sage are cut from the same cloth, as they both fundamentally function from a place of wisdom: when trying to determine the future, they reflect *back* at the past as their reference. For the wise, the focus is not on looking for novel outcomes, but rather on identifying pre-determined possibilities that may reappear. It is no wonder that when the wizards and sages of Egypt were tasked with interpreting dreams, they would have to look back at a manual of pre-defined outcomes. To them, the possibilities were limited to the pages of an instruction booklet.

> *The ancient Egyptian manual of dreams contains over 200 interpretations. In each horizontal line that follows, a dream is described, and the diagnosis 'good' or 'bad'.[4]*
>
> THE JOURNAL OF DREAM RESEARCH

Pharoah, however, required more than just a rehashing of pre-existing interpretations from a textbook. He required vision and creativity – the hallmarks of Yosef the *dreamer*.

> *An increased awareness to dreams increases creativity through*
> *a loosening of stereotyped thinking patterns.*[5]
>> THE JOURNAL OF CREATIVE BEHAVIOR

Further, such creativity and vision can only truly come from a place where *beauty* is appreciated.

> *Evaluation of creativity always requires a judgement of*
> *beauty. Beauty is not the goal of creativity; it is its essential*
> *component.*[6]
>> THE ROYAL SOCIETY OF ART

> *Appreciation of beauty has played an especially important*
> *role in the flourishing of human beings.*[7]
>> THE JOURNAL OF POSITIVE PSYCHOLOGY

We already know that Yosef was no stranger to dreams, but he was definitely no stranger to beauty, either.

> *The daughters of Egypt would step upon the wall to gaze at*
> *Yosef's beauty. (49:22)*

> *"Yosef was of beautiful form, and fair to look upon." (39:6)*
> *– When the women saw Yosef, they could not turn their*
> *eyes from him … being so deeply absorbed in admiring*
> *his beauty.*[8]
>> AVRAHAM IBN EZRA

> *"Yosef was seventeen years old … and he was a youth." (37:2)*
> *– Yosef would spiff up his eyes, pirouette on his heels, fix*
> *his hair, so that he would look beautiful.*[9]
>> MIDRASH

Yet one might ask, is *beauty* actually important to God, to Torah, to Yisrael?

If one goes out into the fields and sees the trees in bud and the flowers in bloom, one says, "Blessed are You, Lord our God, King of the Universe, Who has made a world lacking nothing, and has produced beautiful creatures and trees in order to delight."[10]

RAMBAM

Ten portions of beauty came down to the world and Yerushalayim took nine.[11]

Three things can provide a man with comfort: a beautiful home, a beautiful wife, and beautiful furnishings.[12]

TALMUD BAVLI

Beauty and creativity are expressions of God, expressions of reality, expressions of Existence itself.[13]

RABBI JOSEPH DWECK

While Egypt's wizards and sages needed to look *back* to desperately search for answers, it was Yosef that looked *ahead* to creatively find them. While wisdom operates within the scope of possibility, it is only beauty that can broaden that scope.

Wisdom is the abstract of the past, but beauty is the promise of the future.[14]

OLIVER WENDELL HOLMES

It was this appreciation of beauty that ultimately gave Yosef his visionary ability to think outside the box, to reach the heights of leadership, and to sow the future fertility of Egypt.

The ideological descendants of Yosef appreciate that very same beauty today, and they constantly look towards the future because of it.

Judaism is a journey to the future… Jews look forward more than they look back.[15]

RABBI JONATHAN SACKS

It is no wonder that those who were instrumental in formulating the future vision of our people shared a deep appreciation for the divinity within beauty.

> *When I lived in London, I would visit the National Gallery, and the paintings that I loved the most were those of Rembrandt. In my opinion, Rembrandt was a saint. When I first saw Rembrandt's paintings, they reminded me of the rabbinic statement about the creation of light.*[16]

> *The beautiful arrangement of life, every preparation for the intensification of a person's aesthetic sense, blazes paths for higher lights to appear from the higher spiritual treasury, which flows without interruption, and desires to spread to its fullest in every place which it finds ready for it.*[17]
>
> RABBI AVRAHAM YITZHAK KOOK

Miketz reminds us that by appreciating beauty – that timeless expression of Existence itself – we will ultimately broaden the horizons of possibility. Whether it is the selfless beauty of Torah or Creation, we must constantly strive to seek what the Psalmist seeks ...

> *One thing I ask from God, this is all that I seek...to gaze on the beauty of God.*[18]
>
> TEHILLIM

References

1. Yong Lu, *A theological, ancient Hellenistic, and psychological look at the dreams of Pharaoh's chief cupbearer and chief baker*, International Journal of Dream Research, Volume 9, No. 1
2. Aryeh Klapper, *Torah Leadership*, Miketz
3. Bahya Ben Asher, Commentary to Bereshit 41:8
4. Yong Lu, *A theological, ancient Hellenistic, and psychological look at the dreams of Pharaoh's chief cupbearer and chief baker*, International Journal of Dream Research, Volume 9, No. 1
5. Mauricio Sierra-Siegert, *Minding the Dreamer Within*. The Journal of Creative Behavior
6. Alla Tkachuk, *Creativity & Aesthetics*, The Royal Society of Art. Available online at: https://www.thersa.org/discover/publications-and-articles/rsa-blogs/2018/09/creativity-and-aesthetics-transforming-the-future
7. Phillip Steiner and Rhett Diessner, *Interventions to Increase Trait Appreciation of Beauty*, The Journal of Positive Psychology
8. Avraham Ibn Ezra, *Sefer haYashar*, Vayeshev 15
9. Bereshit Rabba 84:7, Rashi 37:2
10. Rambam, *Mishneh Torah*, Hilkhot Berakhot 10:13
11. Kiddushin 49b
12. Berakhot 57b
13. Joseph Dweck, *Vayesheb 5763*, Audio Shiur available on 'RJD' application on the App Store
14. The Complete Poetical Works of Oliver Wendell Holmes
15. Jonathan Sacks, *A Judaism Engaged with the World*. Available online at: http://rabbisacks.org/a-judaism-engaged-with-the-world/
16. Avraham Yitzhak Kook, *The Jewish Chronicle*, 9 September 1935
17. Avraham Yitzhak Kook, *Arpelei Tohar*, p. 9
18. Tehillim 27:4

vayigash

ויגש

Vayigash – Conscious Integration

It is no coincidence that the reading of *Vayigash* regularly falls around the time of Hanukkah. From Yosef to the Maccabees, the defining question of both stories remains the same – to assimilate or not to assimilate?

After escaping from the depths of despair in an Egyptian jail, to reaching the pinnacle of power in Egyptian government, Yosef is now ready to finally reveal himself to his brothers. Now that family harmony is back on the agenda, surely the plan is to return home?

> *Hurry and go up to my father and say to him, "Thus says your son Yosef: God has made me lord to all Egypt. Come down to me, do not delay.*
> *And you shall dwell in the land of Goshen and shall be close to me – you and your children and your grandchildren, your flocks and your cattle, and all that is yours." (45:9-10)*

Yosef is clearly staying put.

After all, Yosef has taken life in Egypt very seriously! His new name, his children's names, and even his new apparel all seem to suggest a Yosef that is falling victim to the perils of assimilation.

> *Pharoah took off his ring from his hand and put it on Yosef's hand and had him clothed in fine linen clothes and placed the golden collar round his neck. (41:42)*
>
> *Pharaoh gave Yosef the [Egyptian] name Zaphenath-Paneah... (41:45)*
>
> *Yosef named the first-born 'Manasseh', meaning 'God has released me from all the debt of my hardship, and of all my father's house. And the second he named 'Ephraim', meaning*

> *'God has made me fruitful in the land of my affliction.'*
> *(41:51-52)*

As if this was not enough, he demands his brothers to participate in this assimilation too.

> *Yosef did not want his brothers to be as immigrants in the*
> *country. He purchased homes for them, and provided them*
> *with plantations and vineyards.*[1]
>
> RAMBAN

We can now fast forward to the Hanukkah story, and we see a similar situation arising from another foreign culture – Greek.

The Maccabean war turns out initially to have been a Jewish civil war. On one side of the Jewish divide was a powerful entity primed to rid themselves of their Jewish heritage and wholeheartedly follow the common brand of Greek Hellenism, which had already been accepted by the surrounding regions. This group of ashamed Jews wished to *"disguise their marks of circumcision"* and *"repudiate the holy covenant"*.[2]

The Maccabees, originally a meagre group of rebels, took control of the other side of the Jewish divide in this civil war. This opposing group of traditionalist Jews were a population committed to the Jewish covenant and the traditions of their elders.

When the Maccabees and the traditionalist Jews came out as victors, they did something unique and unparalleled in the annals of Judaism: they memorialised a battle victory by establishing a fixed annual observance in the Jewish calendar. Until then, it was common for the Greeks to institute a day for this type of celebration. Further, in choosing the kindling of lights as the distinguishing ritual of their celebration, the Maccabees were replicating another classic Greek custom.

What the Maccabees did in adopting these Greek traditions seems to be as equally concerning as Yosef's adoption of Egyptian life. It seems as though our cherished ancestors in both of these stories have fallen victim to the virus of *assimilation* – the curse word of Jewish life in exile *(galut)*. Or have they?

> *The word 'assimilate' has two quite contrary meanings...*
> *In its primary sense, assimilate means 'to take in and*
> *appropriate: absorb into the system.'*
> *Only in its tertiary definition does it mean 'to become*
> *assimilated'.*[3]
>
> RABBI MATIS WEINBERG

History, and the dictionary, show us that there are two forms of assimilation. One form is characterised by the eagerness to rid oneself of Jewish identity and practice, and to entirely replace it with a foreign culture. The other form looks for opportunities to integrate, while absorbing foreign concepts in order to enhance Judaism as a whole. The latter was the assimilation of Yosef, and the assimilation of the Maccabees.

It requires only a cursory look at Judaism to discover how embedded foreign concepts and languages are in the bastion of Jewish legal codes, rabbinic dialogues, and even our poetry.

> *Rabbinic books are full of Greek words, rabbinic ideas and*
> *institutions are denoted by Greek terms.*[4]
>
> SAUL LIEBERMAN

> *A rabbinic identity emerges in which the rabbis saw themselves*
> *as part of a broad intellectual world, to which Judaism could*
> *contribute and from which it could benefit, and in which they*
> *found productive dialogue partners of many sorts.*[5]
>
> JENNY LABENDZ

> *The deepest and most moving expressions of medieval Jewish*
> *piety would have been impossible without the inspiration of*
> *the secular literature of a competing culture.*[6]
>
> DAVID BERGER

The names of the months in the Jewish calendar have also been appropriated, from our time amongst (even idolatrous) nations.

> *The names of the months [Nissan, Iyar, Sivan, Tammuz etc.]*
> *came up from Babylonia.*[7]

TALMUD YERUSHALMI

> *One of the idolatrous prophets [of Babylonia] was named*
> *Tammuz.*[8]

RAMBAM

Indeed, our *hakhamim* felt that the wisdom amongst other nations even deserves the recitation of its very own blessing.

> *One who sees the wise people of the nations should say,*
> *"Blessed is the Lord, Master of the universe, who gave of His*
> *wisdom to flesh and blood."*[9]

TALMUD BAVLI

And of course, our integration efforts in exile works both ways. Just as Yosef was influential in bringing prosperity to his Egyptian hosts, the wandering Jew has done the same, by offering intellectual contributions, cultural prestige, and economic success wherever he settled.

> *Jews have always gravitated to the capital cities of the world,*
> *and have been able to make their influence, as individuals and*
> *as a group, felt disproportionately.*[10]

DANIEL ELAZAR

> *Judaism was never alien to genuine civilization and culture. In*
> *almost every era, its followers stood at the very heights of the*
> *culture of their day.*[11]

RABBI SHIMSHON RAPHAEL HIRSCH

It is no wonder that Israel, re-established, has advanced so much in so little time. What other nation on earth boasts an amalgamated culture that has been formed by the assimilations of exile? What other nation on earth exhibits a melting pot of intellectualism, music, tradition, and innovation from every continent? The wandering Jew has become the multidimensional Israeli.

Indeed, the fact that the address we regained on the globe retained its relevancy and meaning after all those years was due to that which we – and Yosef – constantly cleaved to throughout our endeavours in foreign lands – God.

> *Yosef said to them, "Don't interpretations belong to* GOD?" *(40:8)*
>
> *And Yosef replied to Pharaoh, saying, "Not I; GOD will give an answer..." (41:16)*
>
> *And Yosef said to Pharaoh, "Pharaoh's dream is one. What* GOD *is about to do He has told Pharaoh." (41:25)*
>
> *And* GOD *sent me before you... (45:7)*
>
> *Yosef said to them, "Fear not, for am I instead of* GOD?" *(50:19)*
>
> *Yosef said to his brothers, "I am about to die, and* GOD *will surely single you out and take you up from this land to the land He promised... (50:24)*
>
> *"When* GOD *indeed has singled you out, you shall take up my bones from this place." (50:25)*

Just like Yosef, the Jews in the diaspora are away from home. However, although the compasses that exilic Jews refer to before prayer may point to different directions, still they are all pointing to the same Place (*haMakom*).

> *The Place is one of the euphemisms for God.*[12]
>
> DAVID WERDIGER

In other words, Yosef's ability to successfully integrate was due to the fact that his dependence upon God never wavered during his time in Egypt – a civilisation that was not short on gods or idols to choose from.

> *Egypt had one of the largest and most complex pantheons of gods of any civilisation in the ancient world. Over the course of Egyptian history, hundreds of gods and goddesses were worshipped.*[13]
>
> ENCYCLOPEADIA BRITTANICA

Yosef's commitment to God was tethered to his Hebrew identity, which was clearly noticeable enough to the Egyptians that refused to sit with him, nor his Hebrew brothers, at their tables!

> *So [the Egyptians] served [Yosef] by himself, and them by themselves, and the Egyptians who ate with him by themselves, because the Egyptians would not eat bread with the Hebrews, as it was abhorrent to Egypt.*[14] (43:32)

This faithfulness (*emunah*) to God is what makes Yosef successful in his foreign environment. And indeed, it is this same faithfulness that allows us to thrive in exile.

> *Our people have been practically everywhere on this globe, with everyone trying to destroy us. And we're not just surviving; we're writing, thinking, and publishing, wherever we are. The Torah has been with us the entire time.*[15]
> RABBI JOSEPH DWECK

In its tertiary definition, assimilation will be pursued by individuals keen on going native and losing themselves by disconnecting from Yisrael. In its primary definition, however, assimilation has helped shape and reinforce our thoughts, our actions, and our way of life.

> *The challenge of the environment stimulates and fertilizes the old faith.*[16]
> HERMAN WOUK

The capacity of Yisrael to foster massive multiplicity and to enculturate itself, while remaining set apart (*kadosh*) and uncompromising about its principles, is evident. It is the wholesome integration of seemingly contrary elements that is characteristic of our people, and it makes our cave of treasures so much busier, so much deeper, and so much richer.

> *Wholeness is not achieved by cutting off a portion of one's being, but by integration of the contraries.*[17]
> CARL JUNG

References

1. Ramban, Commentary to Bereshit 47:12
2. Book of Maccabees, 1:11-15
3. Matis Weinberg, *Frameworks: Genesis*, Vayigash
4. Saul Lieberman, *How Much Greek in Jewish Palestine?*, in Alexander Altman, *Biblical and Other Studies*, p. 332-334
5. Jenny Labendz, *Socratic Torah*, p. 218
6. David Berger, *Judaism's Encounter with Other Cultures*, p. 90
7. Rosh Hashanah 1:2
8. Rambam, *Moreh haNevukhim*, 3:29
9. Berakhot 58a
10. Daniel Elazar, *The Jewish People as the Classic Diaspora*, Jerusalem Center for Public Affairs. Available online at: http://www.jcpa.org/dje/articles2/classicdias.htm
11. Shimshon Raphael Hirsch, *The Collected Writings*, VI, p.120-123
12. David Werdiger, *haMakom as a Verb and Transactional Judaism*, The Times of Israel. Available online at: https://blogs.timesofisrael.com/hamakom-as-a-verb-and-transactional-judaism/
13. Egyptian Gods and Goddesses, *Encyclopaedia Britannica*. Available online at: https://www.britannica.com/list/11-egyptian-gods-and-goddesses
14. Rashi and Onkelos state that it was a hateful and despised thing for the Egyptians to eat together with the Hebrews.
15. Joseph Dweck in Conversation with Jonathan Sacks, *SCA Faith In Our Future*, 11/15/16. Available on YouTube
16. Herman Wouk, *This is My God*, p. 26
17. Carl Jung, *Integration of the Personality*

vayhi

ויחי

Vayhi – Beneath The Surface

Vayhi signals the end of our beginning. Throughout this final portion of *Bereshit*, the giving and receiving of blessings is a recurrent theme.

The Hebrew word for blessing *(berakha)* shares the same root as the Hebrew word for 'pool' or 'wellspring' *(b'raykha)*, aptly emphasising the nature of the ever-flowing and energetic source of life that both words represent.[1]

Since nothing in the world has inherent value, blessings have become a means through which we imbue meaningful context onto meaningless content. In other words, the recital of blessings is Yisrael's daily antidote to nihilism.

> *A person is obligated to recite one hundred blessings every day.*[2]

> *Any item from which one derives benefit requires a blessing.*[3]
> TALMUD BAVLI

By sanctifying the things around us through the acknowledgment of God as the Source of all Existence, our blessings allow us to appreciate what is, and to hope for what can be.

> *In a world where an apple looks like an apple and no more, we must assert its Source.*[4]
> RABBI AKIVA TATZ

It is, therefore, very fitting that a blind and dying Ya'akov at his deathbed chooses to bless his offspring.

> *And Yisrael's [Ya'akov's] eyes had grown heavy with age, he could not see.*
> *And, he brought [the sons] near him, and he kissed them and embraced them. (48:10)*

As moving as this farewell scene is, there is a particular blessing that is rather peculiar. When Ya'akov turns to Ephraim and Menashe, the blessing he makes is as follows.

> *May [Ephraim and Menashe] reproduce abundantly like fish... (48:16)*

How strange. Of all the blessings to give, of all the analogies to make, and of all the mammals to choose from, the benediction for *"abundancy like fish"* seems curious. Other mammals were known to multiply abundantly, so what is so special about fish?

> *Fish are not affected by the evil eye.*[5,6]
>
> RASHI

> *Fish are immune to the evil eye, due to being under the surface of the water and therefore are not visible.*[7]
>
> OR HAHAYYIM

The evil eye *(ayin hara)* is a curse believed to be cast by a person with a malicious stare. By receiving the stare of an evil eye, it is said that the unaware individual is subject to injury, misfortune, and supernatural forces of malevolence. The concept has been embraced by a variety of cultures across the globe, and its origins can be traced back to over 10,000 years ago.[8]

Throughout these years, many preventative measures such as physical amulets[9] and verbal preambles[10] – even in the garb of Judaism – have been invented for protection.

> *Protection against the evil eye was essentially a matter of repelling the demons and evil spirits, and practically all the anti-demonic measures were effective safeguards.*[11]
>
> JOSHUA TRACHTENBERG

Demons ... amulets ... evil spirits – typical ingredients of superstition.

Indeed, many Jews throughout history subscribed to such unfortunate beliefs based on views widely accepted at the time.

> *Although the Scripture and the Rabbis opposed magic and demonology, many Jews, even among the learned and pious, were influenced by the general trend of their times.*[12]
>
> HAKHAM YOSEF FAUR

Are we really meant to believe that, by referring to the evil eye, Ya'akov's blessing to Ephraim and Menashe is superstitious at its core? Is the Torah, with its radical efforts to purge irrationality from our midst, really giving credence to such falsehood *(sheker)*?

Absolutely not.

> *The notion of the 'evil eye' is never explicitly attested in Torah legislation or implied in its worldview ... it is incongruent with Torah's anti-pagan revolution.*[13]
>
> RABBI MOSHE SHAMAH

As many of our greatest *hakhamim* throughout the generations have stated, the evil eye is a symbolic expression of the powers of envy, hatred, and jealousy – the dark by-products of human interaction.

What lies beneath the superficial surface is less a demonic force of destructive doing, and more a psychological malady that can influence negative behaviour.[14]

> *The evil eye is the venomous impact from malignant feelings of jealousy and envy of those around us.*[15]
>
> RABBI AVRAHAM YITZHAK KOOK

> *Extraordinarily beautiful possessions, great successes, superior endowments promote haughtiness and arrogance, prompt jealousy, resentment, hatred, and lead to a host of negative consequences. The "eye" of others, the feeling that one is being scrutinized, may cause the possessor of distinctive possessions to questions his worthiness and "right" to his belongings, rendering him susceptible to unconscious impulses, setting in motion subtle, self-destructive behavioural patterns.*[16]
>
> RABBI MOSHE SHAMAH

It is no wonder that *halakha* – always sensitive to human psychology – has checks and balances in place to prevent the potentially dangerous ramifications of an envious eye.

> *It is prohibited for a person to stand in another person's field and look at his crops, in case he casts an evil eye upon it and thereby causes him damage.*[17]
>
> TALMUD BAVLI

> *Relatives should not get consecutive aliyot, in order to avoid the evil eye.*[18]
>
> SHULKHAN ARUKH

The evil eye becomes a meaningless delusion if it is to be reduced to being a spooky and nebulous demon that attacks the unsuspecting bystander. Instead, it is to be regarded as a psychological phenomenon that is very much a product of our own making – with potentially fatal consequences.

> *God has created a world wherein a person's thoughts have the power to bring damage upon that which one thinks about or focuses upon.*[19]
>
> HAZON ISH

> *An evil desire and jealousy of others will, without a doubt, kill a man. His body will get sick and he will die before his time.*[20]
>
> RAMBAM

When we are able to understand the evil eye in this meaningful way, we come to appreciate the immensely powerful and relevant blessing that Ya'akov gives Ephraim and Menashe. It is a blessing that wishes for his beloved offspring to be spared of the disastrous impacts that an envious eye can have on all persons involved.

> *The envious person gains nothing, the person whom he envies loses nothing, and the only loser is the person who envies.*[21]
>
> RAMHAL

> *The jealous are troublesome to others but a torment to themselves.*[22]
>
> WILLIAM PENN

To become immune to the evil eye, we must concentrate more on ourselves than on others. Indeed, this is why fish is the chosen mammal referred to in Ya'akov's blessing: they spend their lives in their own realm under the sea, detached from concerning themselves with what may occur in other realms, such as dry land. Likewise, we must stay focused on our own realm of values and ideals – unperturbed by the trivialities of others.[23]

> *A heart at peace gives life to the body, but envy rots the bones.*[24]
>
> MISHLE

> *All types of hatred are curable, except that which flows from envy.*[25]
>
> SHELOMO IBN GABIROL

Therefore, Ya'akov's blessing to Ephraim and Menashe cuts at our most ancient and primitive drives to gluttonously glare, to relentlessly resent, and to constantly crave what others have. It is a blessing that is more relevant today than ever before, in a society that is constantly *'logged in'* to watch and hear what others are saying and doing – triggering the dark emotions that lead to destructive states of mind, and impulsive acts of bitterness.

So, what about the demonic forces and evil spirits that were so strongly associated with the concept of the evil eye for thousands of years?

Sometimes, the most rational of phenomenon have the most irrational of garbs.

> *The evil eye is a translation of a profound poetic truth into the language of superstition.*[26]
>
> JOSHUA TRACHTENBERG

References

1. For a thorough analysis of this idea see Aryeh Kaplan, *Waters of Life*
2. Menahot 43b
3. Berakhot 35a
4. Akiva Tatz, *As Dawn Ends the Night*, p. 101
5. Berakhot 20a
6. Rashi, Commentary on Bereshit 48:16
7. Hayyim ben Moshe ben Attar, *Or haHayyim*, Bereshit 48:16
8. Leila Ettachfini, *The Meaning Behind the Evil Eye*, VICE News. Available online at: https://www.vice.com/en_uk/article/59QWD8/i-accidentally-gave-myself-the-evil-eye
9. The now infamous red string wrapped around a person's wrist is said to ward off the demonic forces that an evil eye can trigger.
10. The popular phrase "let it be without the evil eye" is said to ward off the evil eye (*"bli ayin hara"* in modern Hebrew, *"kinehora"* in Yiddish).
11. Joshua Trachtenberg, *Jewish Magic & Superstition*, p. 56
12. Jose Faur, *A Crisis of Categories: Kabbalah and the Rise of Apostasy*
13. Moshe Shamah, *Recalling The Covenant*, p. 446
14. The terms *ra ayin* (Mishle 28:22), *ayin ra'ah* (Pirkei Avot 2:9, 5:19), and *ayin hara* (Pirkei Avot 2:11) refer to traits of miserliness and selfishness.
15. Attributed to Avraham Yitzhak Kook in Chanan Morrison, *Gold from the Land of Israel*
16. Moshe Shamah, *Recalling the Covenant*, p. 447
17. Bava Batra 2b
18. *Shulkhan Arukh*, Orah Hayyim 241:6
19. Hazon Ish, *Hoshen Mishpat*, Bava Batra 21
20. Rambam, Pirkei Avot 2:11:1
21. Ramhal, *Mesilat Yesharim*, Chapter 11
22. William Penn, *Fruits of Solitude*, Part II
23. This idea is extensively discussed in Chanan Morrison, *Gold From The Land Of Israel*
24. Mishle 14:30
25. Shelomo Ibn Gabirol, *Choice of Pearls*
26. Joshua Trachtenberg, *Jewish Magic & Superstition*, p. 55

Acknowledgements

First and foremost, thanks and gratitude are reserved for *HaKadosh Barukh Hu*. My faithfulness to the Covenant *(berit)* has deepened over the years as a result of my increase in knowledge about it, and observance of it. Over the same period, I have experienced life in an increasingly higher definition. This greater clarity of vision has increased my creativity and energy in all facets of my professional and private life. This correlation is no coincidence.

Thank you to my dear wife and best friend – Talya. They say behind every wise man is a wiser woman. I would add: a smarter, shrewder, and more patient woman. Every idea of mine was immediately met with a counter-idea from you, reminding me that if and when I tend to fly in the skies, you'll always be there to keep me grounded.

To my daughter Noa, and my son Joseph – thank you for reducing the volume of playtime while daddy was learning. I truly hope that – in your own individual and unique ways – you will find principles and ideas from our rich heritage to influence you both in your *avodah*, too.

To my strong parents, Goel and Ilana, and my role model siblings, Niaz and Elisha – thank you for providing me with an identity and legacy to learn more and do more, in all fields of life.

To all the *hakhamim* who took the time to read and review these essays – thank you for motivating me with important feedback and words of strength.

Thank you to my Rebbe, the Senior Rabbi of the S&P Sephardi Community of the United Kingdom – Rabbi Joseph Dweck. The Torah you teach around the world enhances so many lives, and addresses so many challenges. Most importantly, it is a Torah firmly rooted in reality, and in the divine principle of *avodah me-ahava* (worship induced by love).

About the Author

Sina Kahen is a Sepharadi Persian Jew. His full-time work is in the Medical Technology and Artificial Intelligence industries. His part-time work involves public speaking and private consulting on strategy, design, and innovation. He is a qualified Biomedical Scientist, and has an MBA from Imperial College, University of London.

Sina lives in London, England with his wife and children.

~

Other books in the *ideas* series will be available from www.SinaKahen.com